Newcomers
to the
United States

Children and Families

The *Journal of Children in Contemporary Society* series:

- *Young Children in a Computerized Environment*
- *Primary Prevention for Children & Families*
- *The Puzzling Child: From Recognition to Treatment*
- *Children of Exceptional Parents*
- *Childhood Depression*
- *Newcomers to the United States: Children and Families*
- *Child Care: Emerging Legal Issues*

Newcomers to the United States

Children and Families

Edited by
Mary Frank, MS in Education

The Haworth Press
New York

Newcomers to the United States: Children and Families has also been published as *Journal of Children in Contemporary Society* Volume 15, Number 3, Spring 1983.

The Haworth Press, Inc., 10 Alice Street, Binghamton, NY 13904-1580
EUROSPAN/Haworth, 3 Henrietta Street, London WC2E 8LU England

The Library of Congress has cataloged the first printing of this title as follows:
Library of Congress Cataloging-in-Publication Data

Newcomers to the United States.

  "Has also been published as Journal of children in contemporary society, volume 15, number 3, spring 1983."
  Includes bibliographical references.
  1. United States — Emigration and immigration — Addresses, essays, lectures. 2. Assimilation (Sociology) — Addresses, essays, lectures. I. Frank, Mary, 1919- .
JV6475.N48 1983 304.8'73 83-8402
ISBN 0-86656-181-1
ISBN 1-56024-120-9 (pbk.)

Newcomers
to the United States:
Children and Families

Journal of Children in Contemporary Society
Volume 15, Number 3

CONTENTS

Introduction   1
    S. Peter Kim
    Katherine Hager Plotnicov
    Mary Frank

CURRENT U.S. POLICY

Contemporary American Immigration and Refugee Policy:
  An Overview   5
    Norman L. Zucker

SOCIAL FACTORS INFLUENCING ADAPTATION

New Perspectives on Immigrant Adaptation   15
    Alex Stepick

IMPACT OF IMMIGRATION ON THE FAMILY
  AND CHILDREN

Immigrant Family Stability: Some Preliminary Thoughts   27
    Geraldine Grant

Children Who Are Newcomers: Social Service Needs   39
    Shirley Jenkins

Intercountry Adoption and Policy Issues   49
    Angela Shen Ryan

EDUCATIONAL ISSUES: BILINGUAL EDUCATION AND RELATED PSYCHOSOCIAL CONCERNS

Language and the Education of Non-English
Speaking Children   61
    Katherine Hager Plotnicov

Self-Concept, English Language Acquisition, and School
Adaptation in Recently Immigrated Asian Children   71
    S. Peter Kim

Problems in the Delivery of the School Based
Psycho-Educational Services to the Asian Immigrant
Children   81
    Yang J. Kim

WILLIAM HIGNETT, *Director, Louise Child Care Center, Pittsburgh, Pennsylvania*

WILLIAM ISLER, *Acting Commissioner for Basic Education, Department of Education, Harrisburg, Pennsylvania*

MARSHA POSTER ROSENBLUM, *Director, Carnegie-Mellon University Child Care Center, Pittsburgh, Pennsylvania*

JUDITH RUBIN, ATR, *Art Therapist, Western Psychiatric Institute and Clinic, Pittsburgh, Pennsylvania*

ETHEL M. TITTNICH, *Adjunct Assistant Professor, Program of Child Development and Child Care, School of Health Related Professions, University of Pittsburgh, Pittsburgh, Pennsylvania*

Newcomers
to the
United States

Children and Families

Introduction

In recent years, the large influx of Southeast Asian, Cuban and other immigrants, refugees, and undocumented aliens has made Americans aware, once again, of a pattern that has been a prominent part of American history, the absorption of people of diverse and varied cultural origins into American society. While the incorporation of immigrants is an accustomed part of American history, this most recent influx became a national concern. For example, in 1980 alone, approximately two million newcomers arrived, which was one and a half million more than the allowed quota. This exceptionally large number of newcomers necessitated changes in federal regulations, in the delivery of social services, as well as causing changes in public attitudes. Because the current problems of immigration are highly complex and controversial, the intent of this issue is to identify how political and social issues affect children and families of newcomers.

The myriad of problems attending the resettlement of newcomers can best be understood within the historical perspective of immigration policies that have changed in response both to the needs of this country as it developed and exigencies of international politics. Norman L. Zucker has provided this historical background. He succinctly summarizes various legal and administrative categories of newcomers along with prevailing controversies in social, economic, philosophical, and political perspectives.

The social climate, and communities, that ultimately support adaptation, assimilation, and acculturation are examined by Dr. Alex Stepick. He examines the adaptation processes of Cuban and Haitian newcomers from a sociological and anthropological point of view and suggests that the success of newcomers' assimilation and acculturation depends not just on individual or cultural traits, but also on the existing national and international social, economic, and political climate.

More specific to the family of the newcomers are their own personal problems. Many are victims of war, political persecution, and economic deprivation. In addition, they face yet another set of prob-

lems. They experience cultural shock, language barriers, employment problems, and alien value systems. Dr. Geraldine Grant
reviews these problems and how they affect family stability by
presenting the development of new roles and responsibilities for
family members.

For families and children struggling with these problems, various
social agencies exist to provide support. Dr. Shirley Jenkins describes the status categories of children as newcomers and the types
of services and supports available to them. She critically looks into
their human needs, the limitations in the present social service
delivery system, and policy issues that exist within the agencies. Included among the social service agencies are those that facilitate and
manage intercountry adoptions. Ms. Angela S. Ryan presents an
overview of the history, scope, and philosophical controversies of
intercountry adoption. She describes the effects of intercountry
adoption on the development of children and their adoptive families,
reviews public policy issues, and provides recommendation for intercountry adoption.

The education of all these children will ultimately determine their
personal success as well as their contribution to their families and
communities. The appropriate educational system for children of
newcomers and their ability to survive in a traditional American
educational system has been the subject of debate for years, and
more recently, the subject of research. Ms. Katherine Plotnicov
places the issue of the language of instruction for non-English
speaking children in its historical context and reviews the current
legal status of educational provisions for non-English speaking
children and the arguments around the issue of bilingual instruction.
Dr. S. Peter Kim reports on his preliminary study of twelve native
Korean gradeschool immigrant children regarding the relationship
between their self-concept, patterns of English language acquisition
and school adaptation and achievement. Dr. Yang J. Kim identifies
and conceptualizes the problems existing in the delivery of the
school-based psycho-educational services designed for the Asian
children.

In summary, the contributors have addressed current U. S. Immigration policy; social factors influencing adaptation; the impact of
immigration on family stability, divorce and its effect on children;
issues surrounding intercountry adoption; and the much debated
educational issues. Beyond identifying these contemporary issues,
included within the context of each article, the contributors provided

exemplary solutions to some problems as well as recommendations for ongoing and future research projects. Finally, it is hoped that through increased public perception and understanding of the newcomers' adaptational process and sociodevelopmental needs, we can facilitate their gainful incorporation into our society.

We are indebted to S. Peter Kim, MD, Director of the Center for Transcultural Development Study and to Peter Tacon, Policy Specialist for Children Without Families, UNICEF, who are both immigrants themselves, and experts in this field, for their editorial assistance in the development of this issue. We are, also, grateful to all the contributors for their expertise, interest, and willingness to participate in this endeavor.

S. Peter Kim
Katherine Hager Plotnicov
Mary Frank

Contemporary American Immigration and Refugee Policy: An Overview

Norman L. Zucker, PhD

ABSTRACT. Contemporary American Immigration and Refugee Policy: An Overview, discusses the fundamental questions of immigration and refugee policy by establishing a continuum of entry legitimacy. The continuum starts from a point of uncontested legal entry and terminates at a point of uncontested illegal entry. Based on the continuum, the author discusses normal-flow immigration, refugee admissions and the existing resettlement system, Cuban and Haitian Special Entrants, the difficulties of separating economic from political motivation in migration, proposals to curtail illegal entry, and the paradoxes inherent in policy because of conflicting pressures and attitudes.

GUARDING THE GATE

Immigration and refugee policy, particularly since the conclusion of World War II, has periodically been an issue of national debate. During the Carter administration, large numbers of Indochinese, Cubans, Haitians and other migrants arrived on America's shores, a

Norman L. Zucker is Professor of Political Science, University of Rhode Island, Kingston, RI 02881. An earlier version of this paper was presented to the National Issues Seminar on Immigration and Refugee Policies for the United States in the 1980s at the Brookings Institution, November 18, 1981. Part of this paper was made possible by a Rockefeller Foundation Humanities Fellowship in Human Rights.

Select Commission on Immigration and Refugee Policy (SCIRP) was established to prepare the groundwork for comprehensive immigration and refugee legislation, and the Refugee Act of 1980 became law. When the Select Commission on Immigration and Refugee Policy delivered its final report in March 1981, the Carter administration had been replaced by the Reagan administration. The new administration promptly created its own Task Force on Immigration and Refugee Policy to reassess the SCIRP report and prepare its own recommendations. During the summer and fall of 1981, the Reagan administration sent to Congress wide ranging immigration and refugee proposals. While no legislative resolution has yet been attained on the Reagan proposals, certain issues are perennial to the debate.

The fundamental questions of immigration and refugee policy are: Whom shall we admit? Why? In what numbers? And once admitted, what should be their rights and entitlements? These complex, interrelated questions lend themselves to no easy and simplistic answers. But an attempt at unraveling the problems can be made by creating a continuum of entry legitimacy. This continuum would start from a point of uncontested legal entry, and terminate at a point of uncontested illegal entry. In the middle would be a large area of judgmental categories. Schematically, the entry legitimacy continuum would look like this:

Legal		Indeterminate		Illegal	
Immigrants (normal flow)	Refugees	Special Entrants (status pending or one-time determination)	Applicant for asylum	Non-immigrant visa abuser	Illegal Alien

The determination of entry status is fundamental because it triggers the responses of the federal government: exclusion, deportation, admission or asylum; refugee status and benefits, or access to federal assistance; legal rights. Where a particular entry determination falls on the continuum is the result of a mix of foreign and domestic policy considerations.

NORMAL-FLOW IMMIGRANTS

The major issues, now and in the future, of normal-flow legal immigration concern the level of annual worldwide ceilings and patterns of preferences and exemptions. While these issues lead to contention between restrictionists and admissionists, the debate over normal-flow immigration is less heated than that over other entry problems. Perhaps this is so because there is control over legal immigration with its attendant domestic impact, and policy can be established through the customary negotiations in the political arena. The refugee, however, is a more troublesome category of legal entrant.

REFUGEES

America's admission of refugees has been, for the most part, grudging and at times deplorable. Refugee admissions, however, from the Truman Administration's Displaced Persons Act of 1948 through the Carter Administration's Refugee Act of 1980 were somewhat more generous. But admissions were determined more by events than by policy. Except for the commitment to encourage emigration from Soviet bloc countries which began in 1951 with the President's Escape Program, our refugee policy has been reactive. Refugees were admitted under special legislation or through the ingenious use of the attorney-general's parole authority. Hungarians, Dutch-Indonesians, Cubans, Hong Kong-Chinese, Asian-Ugandans, and Indochinese were given parole admissions. And to satisfy humanitarian needs, Lebanese and Iranians were given educational visas. A pattern developed: within a few years, Congress would adjust the refugees' status from parole residency, with its disabilities, to permanent residency, making the refugees eligible for citizenship. Refugee admissions, though legal, were not tied to overall immigration ceilings. But admission was just part of the refugee problem, resettlement was the other. The Refugee Act of 1980 provided the congressional consultation in arriving at refugee admission numbers and attempted to rationalize chaotic resettlement procedures and programs.

The existing resettlement system, with the private voluntary agencies as key actors who receive per capita sums for their work, evolved over the years. The present structure began with refugees who came from Cuba after Fidel Castro's takeover. The United States, for the first time, was a country of first asylum for a large number of refugees. And, also for the first time, in December 1960, the federal government assumed significant financial responsibility for the resettlement of the Cuban escapees. That federal input into refugee resettlement remains with us today. Cuban resettlement programs were followed by Indochinese resettlement programs in

1975, and by a domestic assistance program in 1979 to aid Soviet and other refugees not covered by existing Cuban and Indochinese arrangements. By the end of the 1970s refugees were a growth industry. Resettlement had become increasingly expensive and administratively complex. The interdependence between the many public and private entities on federal and state levels required greater coordination. In 1979, in an attempt to rationalize the process of refugee admission and resettlement, President Carter, by executive order, established the Office of the Coordinator of Refugee Affairs in the Department of State. The 1980 Refugee Act statutorily institutionalized the coordinator's office and established within the Department of Health and Human Services an Office of Refugee Resettlement (ORR), which was mandated to develop a comprehensive program for domestic refugee resettlement.

From the passage of the 1980 Refugee Act to the present, ORR has been trying to make the resettlement process more efficient and cost effective. But resettlement is a complex process requiring different approaches for individual refugees and for various refugee populations. Cutting across all refugee populations, however, are certain basic philosophical questions: What, if any, compensatory benefits should a refugee be entitled to and for how long? Under what mix of federal-state-local and private arrangements should refugee services be distributed? The clear drift under the Reagan administration is toward significant reductions in federal funding for refugee-specific services and general welfare benefits. But refugees enter American society with unique problems caused by their uprooting, mental and physical health problems, language and assimilation difficulties, and culture shock. The amelioration of these problems is expensive. Refugees create short-term service and financial drains in health, education, and welfare. In addition they have other impacts on their communities. They may compete for scarce jobs, housing, and remedial services, thereby increasing community tensions. (Why, it is asked, should the Johnny-come-lately refugee get the subsidized job or apartment when the native-born does not?)

Refugees are admitted for foreign policy and humanitarian reasons: since, therefore, their admission serves a national purpose, federal subvention of refugee programs at adequate levels, should continue. Heavily impacted states, however, rarely find federal funding adequate. But this federal-state dichotomy is one facet of the refugee admission mosaic. The refugee admission-resettlement process is circular: successful refugee resettlement eases the way for future refugee admissions; unsuccessful resettlement works to inhibit refugee admissions, because Congress is reluctant to admit refugees who are perceived by the public to be burdensome. The issue is further muddied by the contention that a high profile of successful resettlement constitutes a strong pull factor. While domestically, successful resettlement creates discontent among depressed segments of the population who resent resources and opportunities being extended to newcomers. Some have proposed linking refugee admissions to an adequate level of funding. Others would link refugee admissions to a ceiling on overall admissions. It has been suggested also (and well before the Reagan administration's stress on volunteerism), that the administrative and financial federal role in resettlement be significantly reduced and the slack taken up by the private voluntary sector.

SPECIAL ENTRANTS

Within weeks of its passage, the Refugee Act of 1980 was overtaken by the Cuban push-out, which underscored the unpredictability of population eruptions and the need for the United States to develop a policy of mass first asylum. The Cuban exodus was complicated by foreign and domestic policy considerations. For two decades previously, America had been a country of asylum for Cuban refugees and a well-developed Cuban resettlement program was in place. With the size and suddenness of the Mariel migration, however, no orderly resettlement was possible. Acceptance of Cubans was congruent with foreign policy goals of anti-Communism and anti-Castroism. But never before had America been forced to accept large numbers of unscreened refugees, some of whom would early prove unassimilable. A large and politically viable Cuban community was established in south Florida and the Carter administration, in election year 1980, wanted to capture Florida's electoral votes. The result was a political straddle. Carter promised to "provide an open heart and open arms" for the exiles, but simultaneously invoked his "responsibility to administer the law" regulating the entry of persons.

The outpouring of Cubans also focused attention on another stream of Caribbean migrants, the Haitians, who, in much smaller numbers and without federal resettlement support, had been steadily trickling into Florida. Here too, foreign and domestic policy intruded.

As part of its anti-Communist, anti-Castro stance, the United States had for years supported the dictatorship of the Duvaliers, Papa Doc and President-for-Life Baby Doc. Haiti, a country where the concept of "rights" is rarely applied, is also the poorest country in the Western Hemisphere. To escape political repression and economic privation, Haitians had become "boat people." But when they began arriving on U.S. shores in the early seventies, the Immigration and Naturalization Service (INS) would summarily determine them to be economic migrants and deport them. Challenges to INS's procedures and policies had been entered on behalf of the Haitians, prior to the Mariel boatlift, by churches and civil rights groups. Lawyers for the Haitians accused the INS of failure to observe the aliens' rights and insisted that the Haitians, if returned home, would be subject to persecution. As the Cuban boatlift wound down, federal court Judge James Lawrence King ordered the INS to take no further action against the Haitians until they had an acceptable plan for reconsidering Haitian asylum claims. King squarely dismissed the government's economic migration argument: "Much of Haiti's poverty is a result of Duvalier's efforts to maintain power." The Haitians' "economic situation," he found, "is a political condition."

Facing rising public resentment against both Cubans and Haitians, and a severe impactment situation, and acutely aware of the impending election, the Carter administration tried to neutralize the Cuban-Haitian entry dilemma. The administration decided that the Mariel refugees' motives for leaving Cuba were more economic than political, and that to confer refugee status (with its benefits and concomitant costs) would reward illegal entry and set a dangerous precedent. A new status, "Cuban-Haitian Entrant," was created. This new classification would allow the entrants to remain in the United States and to adjust their status to that of permanent resident alien after two years. (A refugee may become a permanent resident alien after one year.) Entrant status would carry eligibility for supplemental security income, medical, and emergency assistance benefits. State and local governments would be reimbursed for seventy-five percent of the program costs. The outraged Florida congressional delegation pressed through the Fascell-Stone Amendment to the Refugee Education Assistance Act which, to the dismay of the administration, forced the federal government to grant entrant benefits equal to those of a refugee and to provide one hundred percent reimbursement of state and local costs.

INDETERMINATE

The anomalous "special entry" status that was given to some Cubans and Haitians, while earlier Cubans had been considered refugees and other Haitians were expelled as illegals, highlights the problems of definition and interpretation. The 1980 Refugee Act broadened the definition of refugee to include "any person . . . who is unable or unwilling to return to [his] country because of persecution, or a well-founded fear of persecution on account of race, religion, nationality, membership in a particular social group, or political opinion." The definition is simple but the interpretation is a political variable. For years the State Department has accepted the premise that entrants from Communist countries are refugees, while those from right-wing regimes friendly to the United States are economic migrants. Such distinctions are often artificial and arbitrary. Economic and political factors are inseparable in repressive states. Moreover, unapproved departure from a repressive country, more often than not, is considered a crime, and the escapee is subject to punishment upon return.

Argument follows policy and philosophy. The Justice and State Departments, following administration orders, argue that Haitians are economic migrants and if repatriated would not suffer penalties. Amnesty International and church and civil rights groups disagree and press refugee status claims. The State Department contends that Indochinese refugees are political emigrés, and if they are fleeing dire economic circumstance, these are the result of the policies of their governments. But the INS disagrees with the State and calls the Indochinese economic migrants. The United Nations High Commissioner for Refugees (UNHCR) contends the Salvadoran emigrants should be considered political refugees, but the Department of State argues that most of the Salvadorans have come to the United States seeking a more comfortable life, rather than a haven from violence. Frequently, as with many Nicaraguans, when it is desired to avoid a status determination, the entrant is placed in the limbo of "extended voluntary departure."

ILLEGALS

While some aliens become illegal residents by abusing their visa departure dates, the chief concern of those trying to restrict illegal immigration is the "undocumented" person who crosses our borders without proper papers. (Those who seek first asylum in this country also enter illegally and, in the absence of any administrative determination to the contrary, are regarded and treated by the INS as illegal aliens.)

The population of unauthorized aliens currently residing within United States borders has been estimated at somewhere between 3.5 million and six million. Crossing the border is not difficult, and while it is illegal to enter without permission, there are no meaningful penalties for violators. Consequently, border-crossing traffic is not inhibited by fear of detention. The lure of employment triumphs over the temporary impediment of being caught and returned across the border. To staunch the borders hemorrhaging illegals looking for a better life, a number of interrelated proposals are perennially advanced: better border interdiction, employer sanctions, worker identification, and guest worker programs.

More effective interdiction at the Mexican border would require the continuous expenditure of high sums for personnel and equipment. At best it would reduce illegal crossings, not eliminate them. Since the borders would remain permeable to those seeking work, controlling the employment environment is essential. Employer sanctions would penalize those who hire illegals. But determining if a worker is illegal requires a secure worker identification system that does not infringe on civil liberties yet is practical. Implementing both employer sanctions and a worker identification system are politically sensitive issues. A new and expanded guest worker program, if one judges by past experience here and in Europe, would do little to relieve the pressures that propel workers to seek jobs and would place the guest worker in the position of being a disenfranchised subclass in society. Allied to these proposals of tighter borders and better regulated labor conditions is the principle of amnesty for resident illegal aliens. The terms of the amnesty could range from a generous welcome to the institutionalization of a guest worker program under another name.

THE PARADOXES OF POLICY PERSPECTIVES

In immigration and refugee policy it is apparent that sometimes responses and "solutions" become problems in themselves and that our confused attitudes create paradoxes. American foreign policy responses in Indochina led to our responsibility for domestic resettlement of Indochinese. American response to Castro led similarly to resettlement of Cubans. And it is possible that past and present foreign policy moves in Latin America have contributed to emigration. American policies in Haiti contribute to the maintenance of a dictator who perpetuates the conditions that create emigration. Voice of America broadcasts and bountiful resettlement policies, it is charged, pull refugees to our shores. And certainly some of our resettlement policies breed domestic problems.

Resettlement, an inexact art at best, needs to be made analytically sharper, more cost-conscious, and more sensitive to general public concerns and client needs. Resettlement programs, like other bureaucratic enterprises, start small but burgeon and become costly, though not necessarily effective. Horrific examples of excessive costs and negligible results abound: $10,000 for each of 100 Cubans paid to a private contractor to teach them a skill, unaccompanied Haitian minors put in school at $60.00 a day, refugees taking English as a second language for years.

The INS (at best an ineptly administered agency) functioned for years without a commissioner, so that competing political demands did not have to be confronted. Failure to provide leadership enhances bureaucratic drift and inefficiency.

Our policy dictates distinctions between "refugee" and "illegals." With the former we acknowledge the accompanying problems of mental and physical health, job and educational limitations, and the federal government assumes some economic responsibility for their solution. With the latter, we deny such problems and the responsibility falls entirely on the receiving communities. When the national government fails to meet its fiscal responsibilities, fissures in federalism appear. When the state, local, or federal government, insisting still on artificial distinctions, tries to curtail certain of the alien's rights (due process, education), the issue goes to the courts where decisions are handed down, but resolutions are rarely achieved. And when the insistent pleas of the states are ignored by the federal government, governors of affected states are forced to bring suit against the federal government or even, in one case, to go abroad and try to negotiate their own solutions with the sending country.

Our responses that become problems are exacerbated by a confusion and conflict in basic attitudes. We pay lip service to the words of welcome inscribed on the Statue of Liberty, but poetry and reality clash. A resistance to admission comes from such diverse groups as labor unions, environmentalists, population control advocates, the overtaxed, the xenophobic, and the racist. The United States professes a policy of human rights, is a signatory to the United Nations Convention and Protocol Relating to the Status of Refugees, and favors free movement by citizens of all countries. The United States also, by executive order, has entered into an agreement with a dictatorial regime to assist in preventing its nationals from leaving the country; the United States interdicts the escapees in international waters and rules on their claims of political asylum in what the *New York Times* has dubbed "walrus courts." All the while, the United States urges Southeast Asian countries to grant temporary asylum to boat people. Lip service is paid to fair procedures, but the United States Commission on Civil Rights has accused the INS and the Justice Department of discrimination that deprives aliens and citizens of their legal rights. Federal courts have frequently found the government responsible for due process violations. But the administration has sent to Congress legislative proposals designed to restrict judicial review by the federal courts in the asylum process and limit the rights of applicants for asylum.

Problems and paradoxes are inherent in American immigration and refugee policy because we are, as a nation, genuinely ambivalent. Our short range policy will emphasize either admissionist or restrictionist philosophy depending on the state of the economy, the need for cheap labor, or a pressing foreign policy goal. But this is not sufficient. Immigration and refugee policy must also consider the fundamental push-pull factors of international migration. Along with concern over whom to welcome, the United States must also address itself to the issues of world population planning, food resources, and making life more bearable for the great masses of the globe.

SOCIAL FACTORS INFLUENCING ADAPTATION

New Perspectives on Immigrant Adaptation

Alex Stepick, PhD

ABSTRACT. Perspectives on immigrant adaptation have evolved according to changes in the needs of the U.S. labor market and the nature of immigrant groups themselves. For over 50 years, explanations of acculturation and assimilation emphasized individualistic factors reflecting the stratification achieved by immigrants. More recent studies focus on changes in the U.S. economy and the mode of incorporation by immigrants. Immigrant adaptation depends less upon individual characteristics than whether they are incorporated into the primary, secondary, or enclave sectors of the economy.

Miami has become a Latin city. It has also become the principal crucible of current U.S. immigration policy and practice, a vivid example of both its successes and failures. Spanish is heard as frequently as English. Latins have penetrated all sectors of society. They have transformed Miami into the hub of Latin America's in-

Alex Stepick is Assistant Professor, Florida International University, Department of Sociology/Anthropology, Tamiami Trail, Miami, FL 33199.

I would particularly like to thank Alejandro Portes whose indirect help was essential in the production of this article. I, of course, remain responsible for the interpretations and any misunderstanding of his and others' work.

ternational commerce. Credit cards from Ecuador are accepted in Miami department stores. Multinational firms have their Latin headquarters in Miami. Florida's Governor Graham has even called Florida a Caribbean state.

Latins from all of Latin America live, work, shop, and vacation in Miami. However, the refugee from Castro's Cuba initiated the trend in the 1960s and they remain its focal point.[1] The number of Cuban businesses, manufacturers, and professionals is steadily increasing. The successful Cubans have attained good American educations, excellent jobs, lots of money, both Cuban and Anglo friends. They speak English fluently, perhaps with an accent, but more than adequately for business purposes. While most of their consumption patterns may mimic those of the majority of Americans, many still prefer Cuban food; and virtually all watch, listen, and read Spanish language TV, radio, and newspaper. Their capital, entrepreneurial skills, and culture had been welcomed into southern Florida, and it has rejuvenated and diversified both the economy and the culture.

But then came the *Marielitos,* the latest bunch of Cuban refugees. Over 120,000 Cubans came from Cuba's Mariel harbor to South Florida in 1980. Fidel called them Cuba's "worms and scum." Experts estimate that no more than 2-3% were "undesirables," criminals or social misfits. But that small percentage in such a large flow has been sufficient to reverse the image and acceptance of refugees and Cubans.

In November 1980, Miami voters overwhelmingly passed a resolution banning the use of county funds for any language other than English. No more street signs in Spanish, no bilingual instructions in county buildings, nor even Spanish language instructions in hospitals. English is the one and only official language. Thousands of anglos are picking up and moving. *Time* magazine ran a cover story in November 1981 entitled "Trouble in Paradise."

The backlash shocked the Cuban community. The elites especially had convinced themselves that they had been assimilated into mainstream American culture. Now they confronted negative attitudes and prejudice at every turn.

In response to the backlash, Cubans have immersed themselves in profound ethnic self-reflections. The Spanish section of the *Miami Herald* has carried a continuing debate on the definitions and implications of being a Cuban in Miami. Is assimilation viable or desirable? Is a second generation Cuban American still a Cuban?

Should Cubans in Miami abandon their hopes for a triumphant return to Cuba?

Not far from the center of Miami's Cuban community is another Caribbean refugee community, Little Haiti. The Haitians have never experienced the welcome and success of the Cubans. Most are poor and unemployed. They live 10-12 or even more to a room, frequently sleeping in shifts. The Dade County Health Department says that their greatest health problem is malnutrition. There are now nearly 50,000 in Miami, about 1/20 the number of Cubans. They are but a small proportion of the U.S. immigrant population, but they are the subject of a persistent campaign by U.S. authorities to expel them and deter any others from coming. Many of the Haitians have asked for political asylum, claiming they are fleeing repression and terror of "Baby Doc" Duvalier's Haiti. The U.S. government maintains that the Haitians are only economic refugees, no different from illegal Mexicans. Supporters of the Haitians call the U.S. policy racist and ideologically biased. Both sides have been locked in a continual legal and political battle for a decade. Presently, about 1/4 of the Haitians are temporarily covered under the Cuban-Haitian Entrant Program, while the remainder are still in legal limbo.

These two groups, the Cubans and the Haitians, are exemplars of the recent theoretical trends in the literature on acculturation and assimilation which have shifted the focus from individual immigrant traits to social, political and economic factors in the host society. According to these new perspectives, neither the changing image of the Cubans nor the differences between the Cubans and the Haitians is the result of simply individual or cultural differences between the groups. Rather they reflect differences and changes in American society's attitudes and treatment of the immigrants, the socioeconomic make-up of the groups themselves and the immigrants' manipulation of their ethnicity.

For over 50 years, explanations of acculturation and assimilation have emphasized individualistic factors. In Gordon's (1964) culminating theoretical analysis of assimilation, the individual was the starting and endpoint of analysis. Causes of assimilation and acculturation were traits which the immigrants brought with them from the countries of origin: education, skills and occupation, urban vs. rural origins, knowledge of the receiving country's language and customs, etc. Ethnic groups and neighborhoods were depicted as ameliorating institutions softening the adjustment to modern, American life.

The numerous and rich empirical descriptions were often contradictory. Sometimes immigrants tenaciously clung to native, traditional values, resisting absorption into U.S. society (Sellin, 1938; Handlin, 1974). At other times, immigrants were determined to become part of a new, open, and receptive society (Handlin, 1959; Saveth, 1948). Regardless of the results, the causes were virtually always individual characteristics. Even the non-radical nature of American labor unions was attributed not to the policies of the state or the union's internecine feuding, but to the immigrants' "nonmodern" interpretation of labor politics (Rosemblum, 1973).

The nature of American immigration from the late 19th century until W.W. II fit rather well with an individualistic approach. There was indeed individual mobility and differential acculturation. Many second generation immigrants after having grown up in ethnic neighborhoods, adopted American ways, economically and seemingly melted into American society. Those that retained more traditional traits also seemed to be less successful. Of course, many in the subsequent generation attempted to resurrect the ethnic community and the analysts' metaphor switched from a melting pot to something more like a mixed stew.

But in reality this differing and changing acculturation was not simply the result of individual differences; rather, it depended upon the nature of American society at the time and the changing structure of immigrant groups themselves.

American industry at the turn of the century was largely labor intensive requiring a large supply of low wage, unskilled labor. Because of the attraction of cheap land in the still open, developing frontier, industry had a difficult time retaining an adequate supply of native labor (Portes, 1981). They were forced to send labor recruiters to comb the countrysides of Europe attempting to entice peasants to come to America. Hundreds of thousands responded, not necessarily with the intention of settling but usually with the hope of earning enough to improve their welfare back in Europe. Unlike the earlier British immigrants, they were primarily "birds of passage" repeatedly coming to the U.S. and then returning to Europe in concert with the alternating booms and busts of early industrialization (Piore, 1979).

Many did stay and with an expanding U.S. economy, social mobility was possible along with acculturation and assimilation.

But times have changed and with them the nature of America's labor needs and America's immigrants themselves.[2] The U.S.

economy is no longer dominated by labor intensive industry and workers from the world's less developed regions need no coercing to journey to the U.S.

Many scholars characterize the post W.W. II U.S. economy as a dual economy consisting of a large scale, highly productive, non-competitive sector and a relatively small scale, low profit competitive sector.

The non-competitive sector includes large scale enterprises in both the public and private sectors where the primary labor concern of employers is stability of the labor force. Workers are skilled, relatively well paid, and largely native born and white. Restrictive immigration laws since the 1920s have limited immigrants' access to this sector to mainly professionals, such as doctors and nurses, who have firm and stable relationships to their employers. They are usually recruited into jobs in which there is a relatively clear shortage of domestic workers and as such they do not compete with, but rather supplement and complement, the domestic labor force (Portes, 1979). If these immigrants change jobs, it is usually to advance their careers and their social mobility often outpaces that of domestic workers in the same social strata (North, 1978). These are the immigrants who are likely to assimilate into American society most readily.

Conditions of immigrants in the competitive sector are notably different. The competitive sector has lower than average profit margins and a relatively intensive use of labor (Castells, 1975; O'Connor, 1973; Leahy and Castillo, 1977). Jobs require little or no prior training and tend to cluster at the low end of the wage scale. Dead end work, low wages and arbitrary discipline offer no incentive to remain with a particular employer (Wachtel, 1972; Piore, 1973). The principal labor concern of employers in this sector is the maintenance of a stable, low wage labor supply which will not make demands that would erode the enterprises' already slim profits.

Minorities and legal immigrants have traditionally filled these jobs in American society. But following restrictive immigration laws and especially the termination of the guest worker *bracero* program in the 1960s, came an increasing reliance on illegal or undocumented workers (Rosenblum, 1973; Castles and Kosack, 1973). With their narrow profit margins, firms in the competitive sector could not afford to raise wages sufficiently to attract domestic labor nor did they have the capability to lower labor costs by relocating in the developing world. Their only recourse frequently was to resort to undocumented workers whose vulnerability made them a logical supply for low wage labor.[3] Because of these employers' political power (O'Connor, 1973), enforcement of immigration laws for their workers has been lax and a stable supply of workers has been maintained and even increased (Portes, 1977; Cardenas and Flores, 1976; Briggs, 1975; North, 1977; Barrera, 1975).

Although these workers, too, start as "birds of passage," there is an ever increasing permanent community which has even begun to penetrate the non-competitive sector (Cornelius, 1979; Haug and Portes, 1980). The fiercest acculturation battle for undocumented has been the right of their children to a free public education. The State of Texas which wishes to deny them a free education argues that both impose an undue burden and that as non-citizens they have no right to a free education. Advocates argue that undocumented pay as much for public education as anyone else working in the U.S. and that the Constitution confers right to "people" not citizens. The undocumented have lost in the political arena, but still have hope for a judicial victory—the Supreme Court is currently deliberating the case.

According to the new perspectives, a group's political power may be more important in determining their fate than their ethnicity or nationality. Those without power or access to it tend to receive low wages, have little job stability and achieve negligible social mobility. Those with political power may be able to legitimize their legal status, gain access to the economy's non-competitive sector or create an economic enclave of their own, their social mobility (Bonacich, 1976; Galarza, 1964). Mexicans, Cubans and Haitians provide an instructive contrast.

A recent longitudinal study from 1972-73, along with a follow-up subsample, contrasted samples of Mexican and Cuban immigrants revealing the importance of distinguishing immigrants their modes of economic incorporation into the host society (Haug and Portes, 1980; Portes and Bach, 1978; Wilson and Portes, 1980). For the Mexican sample, in contrast to the conventional immigration literature concerning assimilation and social mobility, high education did not increase earnings. Neither did occupational skills brought from Mexico have much to do with U.S. earnings; nor were higher than average earnings associated with the greatest knowledge of English. Interestingly, the minority which found work in the non-competitive sector did earn more even when compared to their peers with the same education, occupation, and knowledge of English.

For the Cubans who immigrated at the same time, the picture is somewhat different. Higher education, skills brought from Cuba, and knowledge of English did yield higher earnings. In general, Cubans had achieved a significant payoff for their past investments in education and occupation, while Mexicans did not. How can we explain the difference?

What in fact distinguishes the Cubans is the large proportion working in enterprises owned by other Cubans. Among the Cuban immigrants were many entrepreneurs and professionals who were discriminated against in the larger American society, but found a ready labor pool and market within their own community. While they do not serve their community exclusively, there is a clear preference for hiring other Cubans and most began by serving their community first. It is also more than just an ethnic neighborhood. It is not only the small businesses which are controlled by Cubans, but enterprises of all kinds and sizes which have expanded beyond the Cuban market (Clark, 1975). Many would fit comfortably in the competitive sector, but they are distinguished by their ethnic owners, employees, and usually their clientele.

The development of this economic enclave was not the product of deliberate economic policies by the host society, but of the initiative and resources of the immigrants themselves. Compared to the immigrants in the competitive sector, those in the enclave have become occupationally heterogenous and many in the first generation have achieved significant economic advancement.

The enclave is by no means unique to the Cubans. It is evident among Koreans, Chinese, Japanese, and in the U.S. was probably first evident among the Jewish immigrants.[4] Indeed the turn of the century immigration of Eastern Europe's Jewish peasantry provoked the same crisis among the earlier more middle class and entrepreneurial groups that is current among Miami Cubans (Portes, 1981). The reaction produced what has been termed "strategic ethnicity," a selective assimilation which promotes economic integration while retaining ethnic traits necessary for group cohesion (Maingot, 1982). The strategic use of ethnicity in contemporary American society can deliver political power to a minority and even transform negative attitudes towards minorities into advantages. Moynihan and Glazer (1976), and Gans (1962) described the roles of competition and conflict in creating and maintaining ethnicity, but they slighted the importance of the ethnic group's manipulation of the competition and conflict in the political arena.

The Haitian boat people in Southern Florida perhaps provide the best example. Ever since they began arriving in 1972, the U.S. government has conducted a ceaseless struggle to return expeditiously as many as possible to Haiti. Yet, the government has been notably unsuccessful. There have been virtually no deportations. The numbers arriving continually mounted, until President Reagan's get-tough interdiction of Haitian boats by the U.S. Coast Guard which began in the fall of 1981.

The Haitians have been so successful in thwarting the government's intentions because of the inconsistencies in U.S. refugee law, policy and practice; and the Haitians' own ability to solicit support as "America's Black Boat People." They have pointed to the U.S. continued welcome to the Indochinese refugees in spite of many experts' beliefs that the bulk of the current Indochinese refugees are "economic migrants" (Suhrke, 1981). There are also the examples of Soviet Jews and other Eastern Europeans who migrate for professional reasons, but are accorded asylum status. While the reasons for the government's discriminatory policies may be more foreign policy based than anything else, claiming that they are racist has a far greater effect.

In the courts and the public arena, the apparent discriminatory, racist component in the government's policy has garnered the greatest sympathy and positive support. A Federal District Court judge in Florida could find no other interpretation than racism for many of the particulars of the government's treatment of Haitian asylum claims (Haitian Refugee Center v. Civiletti, 1980). The judge strongly condemned the government's policies and practices, but he did not provide a final legal resolution to the question of their right to remain in the U.S. He returned that task to the executive branch with orders that the decisions be equitable and just. The Reagan administration, convinced that the Haitian asylum claims had already been within the meaning of U.S. and international law, has appealed the judge's decision and persists in their efforts to expel the Haitians already here and deter others from coming in the future.

The Haitians have been able to use their ethnicity to elicit sympathy and support from a diverse segment of the U.S. population, including positive rulings in the Federal courts. But they still lack the political power necessary to achieve a legal immigration status.

Meanwhile, in many areas the Indochinese refugees have begun to form enclaves integrating considerably better with their host committees than where their concentrations have been too sparse to allow the formation of an economic enclave.[5]

While the examination of immigrant groups' integration into the highest economy increases our understanding of assimilation and acculturation, we should not lose sight of individual immigrants traits. If an immigrant group is to create an enclave it must contain a substantial proportion within the group who have had entrepreneurial experience before immigrating. A migration flow of solely peasants and workers will not produce an enclave economy, although it probably will produce an ethnic neighborhood. The Italian or Polish bourgeoisie never came to America. Nor are the Mexican bourgeoisie presently coming. But the bourgeoisies of the Jews, Cubans, and various Oriental groups have come and spearheaded the formation of their respective enclaves.

Similarly, there must be individuals within the immigrant group with the knowledge of the host society and personal skills to exploit that knowledge and the group's ethnicity. There must be Cubans who know what Hispanic means, even if the concept did not exist in Cuba. There must be Haitians who know that in the U.S. Black is opposed to White, not to Mulatto as it is in Cuba. And even more importantly, there must be leaders to argue these points with force and conviction to the audience of the broader society. Both the Cubans and Haitians have leaders with these qualities. For the Haitians, they have been critical in the legal and political battle to thwart the U.S. government's efforts to expel them. For the Cubans, the leaders have led the way to both economic and political success (Maingot, 1982).

We may depict adaptation then as a product of various forces: traits immigrants bring with them, the social diversity of the immigrant groups, the economic structure into which they become incorporated, and the immigrants' political expertise and power. Adaptation is then a process which spans international boundaries and common conceptual frameworks. The research agenda of the future should consider the processes of development and modernization which differentially encourage individuals and groups to migrate and the processes of labor recruitment, economic activity, and political mobilization in the developed countries which differentially affect immigrant groups. The concern should not be so much with whether a group is legal or illegal, exploited or successful, but with the processes which lead to these states. The new perspectives on adaptation provide a stimulating approach to these issues.

FOOTNOTES

1. Jorge and Moncarz (1980), provide an insightful analysis of the role of Cubans in South Florida. Also, see Jorge and Moncarz (1981); Burkholz (1980).

2. Alejandro Portes has been the leading figure in this field. The most relevant article is Portes (1980) but one should also look at Chapter 2 of Portes and Walton (1981). (1977, 1978a, 1978b, 1978c, 1979a, 1979b, and 1980). The literature with this perspective is rapidly expanding. Those most closely aligned with this perspective and cited below included Bonacich, Light, Castells, Piore.

3. Although it should be noted that there is no evidence that undocumented are paid less than legal immigrants or native workers for doing the same work. Their function is more likely to depress wages indirectly by supplementing the supply of labor in the competitive sector (Portes and Walton, 1981: 57).

4. See Bonacich, Light and Wong (1977), Light (1972), Portes (1981).

5. It must also be pointed out that even where they are forming enclaves, local governments and others still frequently perceive the refugees as an undue burden and strain on local resources. Local governments have lobbied extensively for distributing the refugees more evenly throughout the country.

REFERENCES

Arboleya, Carlos. "The Cuban Community in 1980" Barnett Bank, Miami, 1980.

Barerrera Bassols, Jacinto "Maquiladoras y Migracion," in Margarita Nolasco (ed.), Aspectos Sociales do la Migracion Municipal. Mexico, D.F.: Instituto Nacional de Antropologia e historia/Secretaria de Educacion Publica, 1976.

Beck, E. M., Horan, P. M., and Tolbert II, C. M. "Stratification and a Dual Economy: A Sectoral Model of Earnings Determination." *American Sociological Review, vol 43 (October) 1978, 704-720.*

Bibb, R., and Form, W. H. "The Effects of Industrial, Occupational, and Sex-Stratification on Wages in Blue-Collar Markets," *Social Forces,* vol. 55 (June) 1977, 974-996.

Bonacich, E. "Advanced Capitalism and Black/White Relations: A Split Labor Market Interpretation. *American Sociological Review,* vol. 41 (February) 1976, 34-51.

Bonacich, E., Light, I. V., and Choy Wong, C. "Koreans in Business." *Society,* vol. 14 (September/October) 1977, 54-59.

Briggs, V. "Illegal Aliens: The Need for a More Restrictive Border Policy," *Social Science Quarterly,* vol. 56 (December) 1975, 477-484.

Briggs, V. "Mexican Workers in the U.S. Labour Market," *International Labour Review,* vol. 112 (October) 1975b, 351-368.

Burkholz, H. "The Latinization of Miami," *New York Times Magazine,* September 21, 1980, 46.

Cardenas, G., and Flores, E. "Political Economy of International Labor Migration." Paper presented at the Seventh National Meeting of the Latin American Studies Association, Houston, Texas, November 1977.

Castells, M. "Immigrant Workers and Class Struggle in Advanced Capitalism: The Western European Experiences." *Politics and Society,* vol. 5, 1975, 33-66.

Castles, S., and Kosack, G. Immigrant Workers and Class Structure in Western Europe. London: Oxford University Press, 1973.

Cornelius, W. A. "Mexican and Caribbean Migration to the United States: A Report to the Ford Foundation" Discussion Draft, April 1979.

Clark, J. "The Exodus from Revolutionary Cuba (1959-1974), Unpublished Doctoral Dissertation, University of Florida, 1975.

Edwards, R. C. "The Social Relations of Production in the Firm and Labor Market Structure'', in R. C. Edwards, Reich, M. and Gordon, D. M. (eds), Labor Market Segmentation, Lexington: Heath, 1975.

Gans, H. The Urban Village, New York, 1962, Free Press.

Gordon, M. Assimilation in American Life, New York: Oxford University Press, 1964.

Galarza, E. Merchants of Labor. Santa Barbara: McNally and Loftin, 1964.

Haitian Refugee Center vs. Benjamin Civiletti, 503 F. Supp 442 (S.D. FL. 1980).

Handlin, O. The Uprooted (2nd ed.) Boston: Little, Brown and Company, 1974.

Haug, M., and Portes, A. "Immigrants' Social Assimilation: An Analysis of Individual and Structural Determinants'' Duke University, unpublished paper, August 1980.

Hechter, M. "Group Formation and the Cultural Division of Labor" *American Journal of Sociology*, vol. 84, September 1978, 293-318.

Leahy, P. J., and Castillo, S. "Making It Illegally: 'Wetbacks' in the Social and Economic Life of a Southwestern Metropolitan Area." Paper presented at the Annual Meeting of the Society for the Study of Social Problems, September 1977.

Light, I. H. Ethnic Enterprise in America: Business and Welfare Among Chinese, Japanese, and Blacks. Berkeley: University of California Press, 1972.

Longo, A., and Moncarz, R. "Cubans in South Florida: A Social Science Approach," METAS, Fall 1980, 1,3, 37-81.

Longo, A., and Moncarz, R. "International Factor Movement and Complementarity: Growth and Entrepreneurship Under Conditions of Cultural Variations," Research Group for European Migration Problems, The Hague: The Netherlands, September 1981.

Maingot, A. P. "Relative Power and Strategic Ethnicity in Miami," in R.J. Samude (ed.) The Comparative Acculturation of Ethnic Minority Immigrants.

Moynihan, D. P., and Glazer, N. (eds). Ethnicity, Theory and Experiences, Cambridge: Cambridge University Press, 1976.

North, D. S. Seven Years Later: The Experiences of the 1970 Cohort of Immigrants in the U.S. Labor Market. Washington, D.C., Linton and Co. Inc. (Report prepared for the Employment and Training Administration, U.S. Department of Labor, under Contract No. 20-11-74-21) 1978.

O'Connor, J. The Fiscal Crisis of the State. New York: St. Martin Press, 1973.

Piore, M. J. "The Role of Immigration in Industrial Growth: A Case Study of the Origins and Character of Puerto Rican Migration to Boston," Cambridge, Mass., Department of Economics, M.I.T., Working Paper no. 112, May 1973.

—— "Notes for a Theory of Labor Market Stratification," in Edwards, R. C., Reich, M., and Gordon, D. (eds.) Labor Market Segmentation. Lexington: D.C. Heath, 1975.

—— Birds of Passage: Migrant Labor and Industrial Societies. London and New York: Cambridge University Press, 1979.

Portes, A. "Labor Functions of Illegal Aliens Society," vol. 14, no. 6, September/October 1977, 31-37.

—— "Why Illegal Migration?—A Human Rights Perspective," in Said, A. (ed.) Human Rights and World Order. New Brunswick, N.J., Transaction, 1978a.

—— "Migration and Underdevelopment," *Politics and Society*, vol. 8, no. 1, 1978b, 1-48.

Portes, A. "A Social History of American Immigration," a lecture delivered at Florida International University, November 5, 1981.

Portes, A., and Walton, J. Labor, Class and the International System, New York: Academic Press, 1981.

Portes, A. "Toward a Structural Analysis of Illegal (undocumented) Immigration," *International Migration Review*, vol. 12, no. 4, Winter 1978c, 469-484.

—— "La Inmigracion y el Sistema Internacional. Algunas Caracteristicas de los Mexicanos Recientemente a los Estados Unidos" Revista Mexicana de Sociologia, vol. XLI, no. 4, October/December 1979a.

—— "Illegal Immigration and the International System, Lessons from Recent Legal Mexican Immigrants to the United States," *Social Problems*, vol. 26, no. 4, April 1979b, 425-438.

Portes, A. "Modes of Structural Incorporation and Present Theories of Labor Migration," in Sylvano Tomasi, *et al, International Migration,* New York: Center for Migration Studies, 1980.

Portes, A., and Bach, R. L. "Dual Labor Markets and Immigration: A Test of Competing Theories of Income Inequality," Durham, North Carolina: Center for International Studies, Duke University (Comparative Studies of Immigration and Ethnicity, Occasional Papers Series) 1978.

Rosenblum, G. Immigrant Workers: Their Impact on American Labor Radicalism, New York: Basic Books, 1973.

Sellin, T. Culture Conflict and Crime, New York: Social Science Research Council, 1938.

Suhrke, Astri. "Global Refugee Movements and Strategies: An Overview," paper presented at the "Immigration and Refugee Workshop," Wingspread Conference Center, Racine, Wisconsin, August 17-20, 1981.

Tolbert, C., Horan, P. M., and Beck, E. M. "The Structure of Economic Segmentation: A Dual Economy Approach," *American Journal of Sociology,* vol. 5, 1980, 1095-1116.

Wachtel, H. M. "Capitalism and Poverty in America: Paradox or Contradiction?" *American Economic Review,* vol. 62, 1972, 187-194.

Wilson, K. L. and Portes, A. "Immigrant Enclaves: An Analysis of the Labor Market Experiences of Cubans in Miami," *American Journal of Sociology,* vol. 86, no. 2, 1980, 295-319.

IMPACT OF IMMIGRATION ON THE FAMILY AND CHILDREN

Immigrant Family Stability: Some Preliminary Thoughts

Geraldine Grant, PhD

ABSTRACT: The intent of this paper is to examine aspects of the immigration experience that impinge on the issue of family stability. The meager literature on the socioeconomic background of recent immigrants together with data collected on 150 recent immigrant families indicates that the newest wave of immigrants is, in general, well-prepared for life in the United States. However, the process of immigration stimulates critical changes in behavior which include a redefinition of kin obligations and family life. The trend that emerges from the data is that of an increasingly differentiated and isolated nuclear family. While this type of family is not unique to immigrants, the specific experiences that immigrants have in the United States may make immigrant families more susceptible to various forms of instability than American families. These unique pressures include (1) an extreme economic vulnerability in the U.S. labor market; (2) the rapidity with which male-female roles in the marital dyad must be redefined; and (3) the disjunction that appears to exist between the social status in the country of origin and in the U.S. However, there are also countervailing factors that operate on immigrants that may place a premium on maintaining nuclear family stability. Because wage-labor is frequently unavailable or an unattractive alternative for gaining a livelihood, immigrants often engage in various types of small-scale entrepreneurship. Such ventures depend upon maintaining a high degree of nuclear family interdependence and cohesion.

Geraldine Grant is Research Director, The Ethnic Studies Project, Queens College, The City University of New York, Flushing, NY 11367.

Family instability is increasingly prevalent as a social phenomenon in the United States as indicated by the frequency of divorce, among other indices (National Center for Health Statistics, 1981). The general intent of this paper is to outline some aspects of the immigration experience that impinge on this issue. Undoubtedly immigration disrupts ongoing social ties but the question is whether or not this undermines the ability of the family to maintain itself as a viable social unit. Unfortunately assumptions (explicit and implicit) about both the sociocultural background of immigrants and their experiences in the United States interfere with our ability to identify the factors which either promote or undermine family stability. Immigration is not a new component of American life; over the last 200 years it has accounted for almost 50 percent of the national population growth (Gibson, 1975). The highest levels of immigration occurred in the first decades of this century and this period often serves as a model of what to expect when confronted with a massive influx of persons from cultures divergent from our own. The cultural heritage and class origins of these immigrants—Eastern and Southern Europe, rural and peasant—promoted the development of a perspective that attributed to immigrant's maladaptive and even inappropriate behavior. In fact, this perspective was supported by little empirical evidence then, but nonetheless continues to color our perceptions of immigrants now. Bryce-Laporte (1977) for example, has suggested that the cultural and racial background of the current wave of immigrants not only makes it more "visible" but possibly more problematic in terms of the prospects for assimilation. Such a view ignores the realities of contemporary immigration.

Since World War II, and more clearly after the passage of the Immigration Act of 1965, there have been changes in the immigrant influx that can be briefly summarized as follows: (1) Immigration from Europe, the historically dominant pattern, has declined and immigration from underdeveloped and developing areas, especially Asia, the Caribbean and Latin America, has become the dominant trend; (2) There has been a shift in the occupations of immigrants at the time of entry away from those employed in mining and agriculture to those employed in business, the vocations, professional and technical fields; and (3) There has been an increase in the number of "undocumented workers" or "illegal aliens," that is, persons who abuse their visas or enter the United States fraudulently. The literature on these characteristics, restricted as it is, suggests that new immigrants are fairly well-prepared for life in the United States.

So-called underdeveloped and developing areas have undergone a very rapid process of urbanization and industrialization in the last fifty years, albeit one characterized by a structural, sectoral and regional unevenness (Castells, 1975). Both sending and receiving societies participate in an international economy and exhibit similar dominant ways of organizing economic and political life. Moreover, "modernization" extends to the social and cultural sphere as well (Alba, 1978). Although there are few studies of the regional origins of recent immigrants, the general assessment is that this appears to be an urban to urban movement. Determining the socioeconomic class background of immigrants is more difficult because of problems of accuracy and interpretation. INS data indicates that immigrants are drawn from the pools of professionals and kindred workers, white-collar workers, the petty entrepreneurial class and skilled blue-collar workers (Annual Report—INS, 1977-1978). However, in these samples occupational designation is based on self-categorization and there is no way to verify its accuracy, and many immigrants enter the U.S. as "dependents" for which there is no occupational data. Females frequently classify themselves as "housewives" and this prevents us from determining what their actual skills and qualifications are, or what their work status will be in the U.S. (Tomasi and Keely, 1975). Moreover, undocumented workers are excluded from these reports. Most of the data on this type of immigrant comes from INS apprehensions which is a biased sample. Collecting information on this strata has proven exceedingly problematic even when qualitative methods are employed (NACLA, 1979), but there are indications that "undocumented workers" are not as dissimilar from other immigrants as would be supposed (Portes, 1979).

If standard indices are used to judge overall social status it appears that recent immigrants could be categorized as belonging to a "lower middle class" or "middle class" in the country of origin. Such a designation must be employed cautiously because while "middle class" status has an educational, income and occupational dimension in the United States, it cannot be assumed that these dimensions have the same weight in defining status in other countries. Unfortunately there is little or no descriptive literature on middle classes in developing or underdeveloped societies. The absence of such data means that we have no comparative base; we do not know the role of familial and other types of support systems, the role expectations of either sex in marriage and in the family group among immigrants from specific social classes within specific countries. Without this material it is difficult to accurately predict which areas of life are likely to pose problems for immigrant families; even when problems develop we cannot automatically attribute them to the immigration experience per se or to the retention of socio-cultural forms. Indeed, problems of immigrant family life can also stem from the class position they come to occupy in the United States.

The following is a discussion of the family experiences of approximately 150 recent immigrant households from six countries: Colombia, Italy, Korea, Greece, India, and Israel.[1] The universe from which these cases are drawn is restricted geographically (all within the New York metropolitan area and most from the Borough of Queens), but the regional, educational and occupational profile conforms to the general pattern described above. Birth and residence in a major city was most common, although there was some intragenerational step-migration from rural to urban areas among Greeks, Italians and Israelis. Much of this movement occurred during the respondents early years so that they had spent the major portion of their lives in cosmopolitan urban centers. Educational levels at the time of entry were high, high school or its equivalent as a minimum, and more frequently, some post-secondary technical, university or professional training. The exceptions were predictable by age; those with the lowest levels of education were either very young or older females (50 or more years) at the time of entry. Occupations in the native country were that of white-collar worker, petty entrepreneur, professional, technical worker, skilled artisan and blue-collar worker. Generally, this group appears to be well-prepared to enter an urban setting in which the occupational structure is geared toward white-collar, technical and professional labor. For none was immigration "forced" in the sense of their being political refugees. The overt motives for immigrating were varied but whatever problems these immigrants face we can assume that these are more manageable, either in the short or long run, than the problems they would have encountered if they had remained in the home country. The emphasis is on qualitative analysis, essentially a case study approach based on aggregate data. While not all possible

[1]Funds for this research came from an appropriation from the New York State Legislature in cooperation with the New York State Education Department.

experiences are shown by this group of cases, it nonetheless reveals trends in immigrant adjustment.

IMMIGRANT FAMILY LIFE:
THE REDEFINITION OF RESPONSIBILITIES

Immigration is often seen as disruptive of family and peer group support systems. By implication it is assumed to be an inherently stressful process replete with images of isolated individuals and/or families separated from supportive kin and familiar circumstances. Such images are too simplistic and of questionable accuracy. One of the major intents of the Immigration Act of 1965 was to reaffirm a policy commitment to family reunification, a trend already evident in immigration legislation as early as the 1920s (Keely, 1979). One of the major consequences of this policy is the high proportion of individuals who enter the U.S. as "dependents" of U.S. citizens and resident aliens (INS, various years). This is not, however, only attributable to policy formulations; even among the "undocumented workers" significant percentages are not in the U.S. as single persons but rather as members of a family group (North and Houstoun, 1976). While there is clearly evidence to justify describing this wave as a family immigration pattern there are ambiguities in this characterization. Garrison and Weiss (1979) have argued that the definition of "family" used in U.S. immigration policy is too narrow and too rigid, including in its broadest extension, married siblings and parents. Their contention is that larger kin aggregates are functionally relevant in many donor societies and that U.S. immigration policy should take into account the realities of kin and domestic arrangements rather than *a priori* defining them. Unfortunately there is little literature on the types of families immigrants originate from or what role extended networks of kinsmen play. On the one hand this research has indicated that larger kin aggregates operate in a variety of contexts in the donor society. On the other hand it suggests that immigration redefines kin obligations and family life.

Immigration apparently requires the mobilization of kin ties at home. Decisions to immigrate were rarely made by single individuals; a broad range of family members were directly or indirectly involved in the decision and its implementation. Significantly, one of the more common immigration patterns was, at least initially, that of solitary individuals, relatively young (under the age of 30), and unmarried. The rationale of this pattern from the perspective of the sending family is that these persons have few family responsibilities and their absence minimally disrupts family life. However, there were a number of cases in which husbands immigrated alone temporarily leaving dependents behind. Other family members were called upon to meet the immigrant's obligations in his absence. Although wives sometimes had to adjust their living arrangements, separations were viewed by neither husbands nor wives as overly problematic or even unusual. Disagreement, when it occurred, centered on the length of separation rather than its existence. When males left they frequently could not precisely define how long before the family would be reunited or, in some cases, the permanency of the move. These decisions were made subsequently and plans then implemented for reuniting husband with wife. Although none of the households exemplified adult married females without husbands or children, in several instances, wives joined husbands in the U.S. leaving young children with various relatives. Respondents did not express dissatisfaction with the quality of care their children received but rather with the length of a separation that ranged from one to four years.

For those left in the country of origin, networks of kinsmen fill the vacuum created by the departure of an immigrant. However, beyond this type of support it is not clear what other role larger kin aggregates play in the life of the immigrant and his immediate family. My own previous research on non-immigrant Latin American middle class families showed that one result of modernization is the emergence of the isolated nuclear family as the viable social unit, a process largely attributable to the progressive loss of control of productive property by larger kin groups over several generations. Although networks of real and fictive kinsmen were relevant to a host of life situations there was no resource pooling among extended families in this generation (Grant, 1978). Many of these immigrant families had been wage and salaried workers before immigration but the immediately previous generation had control of real property. In other instances, the liquidation of joint family property immediately preceded immigration.

Although the available data does not permit us to accurately determine the types of families associated with immigrants from specific social classes, it is clear that nuclear families are the norm that emerges in the context of immigrant life in the United States. Figure 1 provides a breakdown of the 150 families by household type. The dominant pattern is clearly that of the nuclear family consisting of

Figure 1: Immigrant Households		
Family Type	Number	Percent
Nuclear	104	68%
Extended	21	14%
Other	27	18%
Total	152	100%

husband-wife and dependent children, although for some it was made up of parents and adult, unmarried children. Extended families, either intergenerational or intragenerational, accounted for a much smaller proportion of the cases. Moveover, among households categorized as an extended family, relatives other than the nuclear unit were not seen as permanent members of the household. Similarly many nuclear family households had at other times other kinsmen as part of the family.

During the first years of residence in the United States immigrants made extensive use of kin and quasi kin relationships in establishing themselves. For some, previous waves of immigrants represented a pool of kin upon whom they could rely. Close and distant kinsmen already established in the United States extended a variety of supports to newcomers (help in finding a job, small loans of money, lodging, etc.). For those without family, instrumental social ties based on common points of origin, situation (e.g., fellow student), or immigrant status were developed to deal with logistic problems. Living arrangements in the first year or two included co-residence with immigrant kinsmen, distant and near, renting a room in a fellow ethnic or immigrant household, sharing an apartment with other immigrants from the same or similar geographic areas. However, with the possible exception of aged parents (for whom there was no other responsible party in the home country) an attitude of permanent responsibility and/or mutual economic obligation was notably absent.

Not only was the expectation of permanency lacking but also the desire. In some cases covert and overt conflict over the allocation, distribution, and utilization of family resources was a precipitating cause for migrating. Frequently, respondent's expressed reason for immigrating was to be on one's own, pursue individual talents and maximize the individual's, as opposed to the family's interests. Although many sent money to kinsmen in the native country this was an occasional and erratic, not consistent, occurrence. These attitudes and behaviors contrasted with those informants reported to have shown towards kinsmen before immigrating. It could be argued that a major reason for immigrating is to sever ties with or mediate the impact of family obligations on the individual. If immigrants are separated from kin some of this separation may indeed be welcomed. Immigration apparently provokes a temporary broadening of family interactions both here and at home, but this breadth is not matched by a sense of significant mutual obligation. Rather the opposite occurs; the scope of the permanent functional kin unit narrows considerably. For immigrant families immigration not only redefines the obligations to larger kin aggregates but also the rights and responsibilities of the marital dyad.

Although a nuclear family characterized by exclusive male responsibility for generating household income and female responsibility for domestic tasks, represents an ideal version of American family life, if it ever had much reality for wage earning families, it was restricted to a brief and specific period of American history, the post World War II affluent society. Increasingly maintaining a satisfactory standard of living requires two wage earners. Immigrant households are no exception. For females, immigration brings with it active and sustained employment in contrast to their experiences in the native country. Women overwhelmingly described themselves as "housewives" and an examination of their work history showed this to be an accurate description. Few held jobs before immigrating although there was some variation from country to country. Asian Indians, even the most highly educated, rarely had worked outside the home; after marriage, and even before, they were expected to confine their activities to the domestic realm. In contrast, Colombian women often worked before marriage and after, until the birth of the first child. Those women who had operated some type of business indicated that it was frequently based in the home and overlapped with domestic roles. The INS data on female dependents clearly does not reflect the role they come to play in the U.S. labor market.

For both sexes, employment in the United States presents a unique set of problems which bear on the issue of family stability. As previously discussed one of the salient characteristics of new immigrants is that, on a whole, they appear to be well prepared to enter the urban labor market. However well prepared the immigrant may be, there is a large gap between preparation, expectation, and actual experience. In total the dominant trend for *first* job experience was employment in the service and manufacturing sector in low-skill jobs in non-union factories, low paying service jobs (e.g., domestic work), low-level positions in retail and wholesale trade, and low-level clerical positions. Over 80 percent of the cases were employed in these areas, in what is referred to as the secondary labor market (Piore, 1976; Edwards et al., 1975) characteristically defined as an unskilled labor market (cf. Sassen-Koob, 1979). Historically women, youth and minorities have clustered in these industries and sectors of the economy, although increasingly native workers are unwilling to take these jobs because the extension of social welfare services provide a viable alternative to employment in what are low wage and unstable positions (cf. Kuhn, 1978). What native minorities, youth and women are unwilling to do, immigrants of both sexes, at least initially, must do.

For the majority, immigration was found to be a great leveler of socioeconomic differences, great and small. Labor market credentials acquired in the country of origin were not directly transferrable to the U.S. labor market except among very specific categories of professionals (particularly medical physicians). Individuals who attempted to find employment commensurate with what they saw as their qualifications, found that "immigrant" status meant that their credentials were not regarded as "culturally" valid. Even for the other 20 percent of our cases, those who initially found jobs in the primary labor market (many of whom entered under the skilled manpower provisions of the immigration acts), foreign work experiences and education were suspect and downgraded. Although for subsequent jobs many found (by a variety of yet undetermined means) more acceptable employment, job dissatisfaction was high and there were indications of underemployment. Discrimination by co-workers and supervisory personnel on the basis of language deficiencies or merely foreign status (not race, sex or national origin) was often alleged to interfere with job and career advancement. Because of these forms of discrimination, particularly the lack of recognition of work credentials, various types of entrepreneurship become a more viable alternative to wage labor. Businesses are small-scale operations, rarely relying on hired labor but rather on the collective efforts of both adult and adolescent children.

CONCLUSION

The general trend that emerges from the data is that of an increasingly differentiated and isolated nuclear family household. This situation is not unique to immigrants and probably reflects their overall socioeconomic class position in the United States. What is unique to immigrants is the exceptional precariousness of their economic position and the rapidity with which roles must be redefined. The disjunction between socioeconomic status at home and actual experiences in the U.S. suggests that, at least initially, many experience a form of downward mobility. Whether or not males suffer a decline in self-esteem as a result is a complicated question that requires a careful examination of status categories and how they are defined at home and the U.S. Clearly the jobs available to immigrant males require female work partners if a minimally satisfactory standard of living is to be achieved. This requires a redefinition of roles. According to informants, domestic tasks in the country of origin were often shared with female relatives and/or shared with hired help, maids and other family retainers. In the U.S., females must take on a host of new responsibilities and roles for which they are ill-prepared and unaccustomed. As a result, friction between husbands and wives is undoubtedly more common, a fact that has been commented upon in the ethnic press.

The original intent of this paper was to outline some aspects of immigration that bear upon the issue of family stability. Immigration clearly entails the redefinition of sex roles and possibly the very organization of families. Divorce was more prevalent than it was in the country of origin, where it was generally not regarded as an acceptable cultural alternative. However, we cannot say whether or not the pressures immigrants face place them in a greater risk situation than other American families who occupy an analogous social and economic position. For families in general, the labor demands placed on two adult individuals have increased, and undoubtedly this factor, coupled to the redefinition of roles, ambiguities in these roles and changing expectations, have contributed to the spiraling divorce rate. On the one hand immigrants are clearly disadvantaged in their ability to deal with these pressures. For one, their economic vulnerability is patent; for another, the readjustment of role expectations for husbands and wives is extreme. On the other hand, there are characteristics that may contribute to family stability. The frequency with which other relatives, either as visitors from abroad or as temporary members of the household, are incorporated into the family, eases somewhat the problems of child care experienced by working mothers. Moreover, because wage and salary alternatives are frequently unacceptable or unavailable, various entrepreneurial options become attractive. The organization and operation of small-scale business depends on the maintenance of family cohesion and the exploitation of family labor. A productive research focus for the issue of family stability among immigrants would be a comparison of the way in which entrepreneurial and wage labor immigrant households handle the pressures of their new lives.

REFERENCES

Alba, F. Mexico's international migration as a manifestation of its development pattern. *International Migration Review*, 1978, *12*, 502-13.

Bryce-Laporte, R. Visibility of the new immigrants. *Society*, 1977, *6*, 18-22.

Castells, M. Immigrant workers & class struggle in advanced capitalism. *Politics & Society*, 1975, *5*, 33-66.

Edwards, R. Labor market segmentation. Lexington, Mass.: D. C. Heath, 1975.

Garrison, V. Dominican family networks and U. W. immigration policy: A case study. *International Migration Review*, 1979, *XIII* (2), 264-283.

Gibson, C. The contribution of immigration to the United States population growth 1790-1970. *International Migration Review*, 1975, *9*(2), 151-177.

Grant, G. *A path to marginality: The rise of a provincial Chilean middle class.* Unpublished doctoral dissertation, 1978. The Graduate Center, City University of New York.

Immigrants admitted by country or region of birth and major occupation group: Table 8. Annual Report: *Immigration and Naturalization Service.* Washington, D.C.: Superintendent of Documents, 1976-77.

Keeley, C. The United States of America. In D. Kubat (Ed.), *The Politics of Migration Policies.* New York: Center for Migration Studies, 1979.

National Center for Health Statistics. *Provisional Statistics, Monthly Vital Statistics Report.* Washington, D.C., 1981.

Immigrant Workers in New York City. *North American Congress on Latin America*, 1979, *XII* (6).

North, D., & Houstoun, M. *The characteristics and role of illegal aliens in the U.S. labor market: An Exploratory study.* Washington, D.C.: Levitan, 1976.

Piore, M. Notes for a theory of labor market stratification. In Gordeon et al. (Eds.), *Labor Market Segmentation.* Lexington, Mass.: D. C. Heath, 1976.

Portes, A. Illegal immigration and the international system, lessons from recent legal Mexican immigrants to the Unites States. *Social Problems,* 1979, *26*(4), 425-438.

Sassen-Koob, S. Immigrant and minority workers in the organization of the labor process. *Journal of Ethnic Studies,* 1979, *7*.

Tomasi, S., & Keeley, C. *Whom have we Welcomed? The Adequacy and Quality of U.S. Immigration for Policy Analyses & Evaluation.* New York: Center for Migration Studies, 1975.

Children Who Are Newcomers:
Social Service Needs

Shirley Jenkins, PhD

ABSTRACT. Children who are newcomers to the United States fall into several status groups, including refugees, entrants, immigrants, and undocumented aliens. Some come with their families and others are unaccompanied minors. Their needs for supports and services range from food and shelter, to language education and help in acculturation. These children and their families do not fit neatly into our categorical service system. In addition to being newcomers, the majority are "visible ethnics," facing problems of prejudice and racism. As time runs out for federal reimbursement for refugee support many new arrivals may seek a share of the shrinking welfare budget.

Immigrants and refugees cross boundaries in their search for new homelands. Social agencies which help immigrants and refugees also span boundaries, but boundaries of service systems rather than of nations. Such agencies must interact with governmental, religious and ethnic groups, and their service plans depend heavily on the immigrant status of their clients. In addition, the process is affected by the political climate and the issues of international foreign policy which lead to the movements of people from one country to another. These complications mean that services for newcomers tend to be specialized and categorical, and agencies which are involved tend not to be in the mainstream of our national social welfare system.

This article seeks to locate minors who are newcomers, regardless of status, in the service delivery system. Rather than deal with the details of complex programs, the goal is to categorize groups, discuss social provision, describe service examples, and briefly suggest some policy issues.

There are many ways of classifying newly arrived persons, such

Dr. Jenkins is Professor of Social Research at the Columbia University School of Social Work, Columbia University, New York, NY 10027. Her most recent book is *The Ethnic Dilemma in Social Services* (Free Press, 1981).

as age, sex, country of origin, language, and religion, among others. But to place young newcomers in the social service system it may be most useful to sort them into six main groups. There are those who arrive without families or adult guardians, the "unaccompanied minors." They may be of all ages from infancy through adolescence, and initially they require substitute care in foster homes or group or institutional placements. Some are classified as "refugees," and some as "entrants." Then there are minors who come with their families. They may be "entrants," if they are Cubans or Haitians who arrived in a specified time, or refugees if they are under the protected status of the Refugee Resettlement Act, such as the Indochinese and the Russian Jews. Refugees may qualify for entitlements of cash support and services for a transitional period, formerly three years. A further group to be considered are children of immigrant families who come on their own initiatives, under the Immigration and Nationality Act, usually for economic reasons or to join family members. If they need help they become part of the mainstream of clients, often of minority background, who seek assistance from the public and voluntary service systems. Finally, the fourth group comprises children of undocumented aliens, the "non-person" minors whose families are without sponsorship or legal status, and who have uncertain access to the most basic programs of health and education. For each of these four groups there are different sets of entitlements, service provisions and social supports.

UNACCOMPANIED MINORS (REFUGEES)

Attention to the plight of minors who were not with families was aroused in the mid 70s, when refugees and "boat people" reached camps of "first asylum," mainly in Malaysia, Thailand, Singapore and Indonesia, prior to resettlement in a third country. In these camps, run by the United Nations High Commissioner for Refugees, there were numbers of youngsters without families. In addition, after transport to the United States and assignment of family groups to sponsors, there was significant separation of minors from what had previously appeared to be family units. This situation led to the establishment in December 1978 of a definitive policy for priority admission of unaccompanied minors and their subsequent care and support.

Two national sectarian voluntary agencies, the United States Catholic Conference and the Lutheran Immigration and Refugee Service, both of which have ongoing foster care systems, administer the resettlement program for minors under 17 years. In describing this effort to State administrators, the specifications issued on February 6, 1979 of the Department of Health, Education and Welfare (now Health and Human Services) mandated some principles relative to the delivery of services to these youngsters. For example, it was specified that, "The same range of child welfare benefits and services available in foster care cases to other children must apply to lawfully admitted unaccompanied Indochinese minors." Another specification is "The children are not to be placed for adoption." Still a third requirement is that: "Consideration must be given to 'acculturation' through: (a) integration of the Indochinese child with American culture; (b) preservation of his or her ethnic identity; (c) reunification with family members and contact with his or her own ethnic community."

These three specifications, sound as they may be in principle, illuminate some of the dilemmas faced in service delivery. In the United States, foster care services not only vary from State to State, but from agency to agency. Is the Indochinese child entitled to parity with the best, or with the worst, of foster care? Adoption is indeed inappropriate for this group, but the typical American foster care program is committed to the concept of permanency, with early decisions for either return to biological parents or to adoption. Finally, to undertake both integration with American culture and preservation of ethnic identity is indeed a challenge.

Indochinese minors who arrived in this country needed everything: food, clothing and shelter; language and acculturation; and emotional supports. Different substitute programs for these children functioned at varying levels, and a single assessment is difficult. In response to public concerns about the service programs, the Citizens Committee for Children undertook two independent studies of such programs in New York State, first in 1979 and again in 1980, with published reports issued for each the following year. In the initial study (1980), they visited seven programs serving about 186 youngsters. They were generally satisfied with the physical care of the Indochinese minors, and the dedication and concern of staff. Criticism was expressed at the time of the initial review, of the general secrecy which seemed to pervade the operation, the isolation of the settings, and the institutional nature of the placements. By the time of revisits a year later, the swing had been to foster family care, much of it arranged by direct airplane-to-home placement (1981). In ''one-on-one'' settings where newly arrived children who were unable to communicate in English were separated from others of their group, it was difficult for foster parents to establish relationships. Foster family care is typically not the placement of choice for American adolescents, and for these Asian youngsters it seemed to be particularly inappropriate.

Among the problems identified by the Citizens' Committee review were differences in cultural patterns, withholding of affection by the youth, and impatience with the role of being treated as dependent children on the part of the minors. Since about 85 percent of the group was from 15-18 years, and had been on their own after wartime displacement, they fit more into the young adult than the child category. Although the dependent status of these adolescents was real, and foster care a way of buying time for adaptation, the psychosocial needs of this group were of a different order. Less isolation, more emphasis on vocational training, small reception centers, group living, and settings which provide more chances for group identity were all recommended by the Citizens' Committee investigators.

UNACCOMPANIED MINORS-STATUS ENTRANTS

If the Indochinese minors needed everything, then youngsters from Cuba and Haiti needed more than everything. Because they did not arrive after prior screening in another country, they lacked refugee status, and were subject to detention and threats of repatriation. For the thousands of Cubans and Haitians who simply landed on the Florida shores from June to October 1980, a new interim category of ''entrants'' was devised, as specified in the Fascell-Stone amendment to the Refugee Education Assistance Act (P.L. 96-422). This provision extended social service benefits applicable to refugees to entrants, at least until the latter's status is clarified.

For the unaccompanied minors among the entrants, there was much disorganization and unsatisfactory care. Several hundred Cuban minors, for example, were sent to Camp McCoy in Wisconsin. A social worker employed as consultant to the University of Miami in the Cuban Unaccompanied Minors Program visited the camp, and reported:

. . . A number of barracks served as dormitories where their housekeeping conditions were deplorable with piles of garbage in the sleeping quarters, spoiled food scattered throughout the place, flooded bathrooms and toilets, and broken glass windows which the boys tried to fix with cardboards to protect themselves from the cold.

There was a barracks to be used for schooling, but there were no teachers or educational program of any kind. The complete absence of recreational programs permitted the youngsters to lead a very unstructured kind of life, staying in bed until 10 a.m. and aimlessly walking around with nothing to do. (Ortiz, 1981)

Eventually these children were placed with foster families in Wisconsin and the camp was closed, but the record stands.

Some Haitian children were treated in a more traditional setting. Facilities for about 200 unaccompanied minors were found, one in Florida and one in New York State, both to be run as detention centers. The New York facility, the Hope Farm Campus of Greer Woodycrest Children's Service, in rural mid-New York State, was visited by a group of observers from the Citizen's Committee for Children (1981). Unlike the Wisconsin center, this was found to be clean, well equipped, and with a full program for the adolescent residents. The observers, however, were concerned that there was little in the experience to help in the transition to urban life. In particular, isolation from friends and relatives in the Haitian community could only reinforce the sense of loss and lack of identity of the unaccompanied minors.

REFUGEE CHILDREN WITH FAMILIES

Refugee children who come with families have many needs for services, but they are more concrete and temporary, since parents and kin relate to basic emotional needs. One study of the mental health needs of Vietnamese children in a large refugee camp, for example, reports that there is a "capability of Southeast Asian children to cope with stresses of migration when supported by their families" in contrast to the "vulnerability of children separated from families" (Harding, 1977).

Even given closeness of relatives, however, there are formidable problems, the first being reception and resettlement. The umbrella agency in the United States which oversees this process is the American Council on Voluntary Agencies, which works in conjunction with the U.S. government after the screening of refugees by the United Nations High Commission for Refugees. ACVA is the administrative and statistical center serving approximately 34 agencies active in the field of foreign aid; of which 10 agencies participate in the settlement of refugees. These 10 include both sectarian and secular groups, such as the U.S. Catholic Charities, the Lutheran Services, Hias, which relates to Russian Jewish refugees, and others. It is the task of ACVA to work with its contracting agencies to assure sponsorship of the refugees who have been screened in the camps or overseas, and to help direct the flow of movement to states and localities. Sponsorship does not imply any financial responsibility, however, since the program is federally funded under the Refugee Act of 1980, and 100 percent reimbursable to the states.

Although there are obvious problems of language, culture, climate and customs, the basic service package actually provides preferential treatment for families and their children in this category. Refugee families without resources, including able bodied men, for example, are entitled to welfare, health services, CETA jobs when available, and this is supplemented by a network of family agencies involved in service delivery and job development.

The American Council for Nationalities Service is one of the constituent agencies of the ACVA which accepts responsibility for refugee groups. Their goals are carried out through a network of member agencies, which are all members of their local United Way. These agencies provide counseling, referral, language, employment, and cultural services to new immigrants. The focus is often on the adults, since there is an assumption that the schools will take a major role in the acculturation of the children.

The comprehensive refugee resettlement program has been generous in entitlements. It initially extended to three years, which was considered to be a reasonable time to achieve self-support. A substantial cut back to 18 months in the time for 100 percent Federal reimbursement has now been projected, as well as other restrictions. The considerable problems faced by refugees including language, acculturation and the shrinking employment market, make this an optimistic projection. Time is already running out for many refugee families, especially on the West Coast, and many have already lost their protected position. In that case the refugees will be in competition with American welfare recipients who are facing reduced benefits and service cuts. One danger lies in the impact of losing their waiver from categorical eligibility, and being subject to a welfare system which gives preference to single parent families. Another problem is the capping of the welfare programs, leaving the system unable to assume support of large new groups of eligibles such as the refugees.

CHILDREN OF IMMIGRANT FAMILIES

There is a double standard in evaluating needs of refugees and of potential immigrants, with unprecedented privileges accruing to the former. Immigrant families cannot enter without carefully documented affidavits guaranteeing that they will not become public charges, and a retarded child or a handicapped family member could cause problems for entry. During their wait for naturalization, many families are uncertain about their legal rights to services, and do not take up entitlements because of fear of disturbing their immigration status.

A second factor to be considered are the demographics of the new wave of immigrants. As noted in the 1980 Census data, the large majority of immigrants of the past decade have been the "visible" ethnics, from Asia, Africa and Central and South America. (*New York Times,* September 6, 1981). This resulted from the abolition of country quotas under the Immigration and Nationality Act of 1965.

For personal social services, as distinct from income supports, the new immigrants will patronize both public and voluntary agencies, and establish their own helping networks which may be related to ethnic associations. The new wave came to this country on the heels of the civil rights movement, and the strong representations of minority people for the right to retain ethnic identity. The benefits of this movement, initiated by Blacks, Puerto Ricans, Chicanos, Asians, and American Indians, should accrue to new immigrants. Furthermore, there is a growing literature on the concept of incorporating ethnic factors in service delivery (Jenkins 1981).

New immigrants may find the ethnic or mutual aid association to be the most responsive to their needs. How such groups relate to each other, as well as how they can articulate with the traditional service system, will affect their potential effectiveness. Coalitions within groups are needed and there are some efforts in that direction. Coalitions among groups, such as between Hispanics and Vietnamese, however, are much further down the line.

CHILDREN OF UNDOCUMENTED ALIENS

"Undocumented aliens" is a euphemism for persons illegally in the United States, without residential, immigrant, or refugee status. The largest ethnic group among undocumented aliens are the Hispanics, in particular Mexican Americans. These are often thought to be single male migratory workers, but in fact a large number are families with children, many of long-time residence. Children in this status have family-based emotional supports, and economic support from working parents. But they lack security, permanence, and social acceptance. Furthermore, they are threatened by the loss of educational and health services, because of their uncertain legal position. In a study of comparative stress among documented and undocumented Mexican families, for example, Salcido found a high stress level for 52 percent of undocumented families studied, but for only 20 percent of legal aliens (1979).

Questions of entitlement are particularly sharp when some members of a family may be documented, and others not. An alien mother, for example, may have a child born in the United States in need of services, but treatment for the citizen child could subject the mother to possible deportation (Ramirez and Haney-Gooden, 1979).

The rights of alien children to an education is a key issue, heard but not yet decided by the U.S. Supreme Court (*New York Times,* December 2, 1981). Responsibility for school support was raised in a Texas case affecting over 11,000 "undocumented" children, when a 1975 Texas law which denied State funds for the education of children of illegal aliens was appealed. Three lower Federal courts struck down the law, with Judge Seals and the U.S. Court of Appeals for the Fifth Circuit concluding in July 1980 that the decision would "harm a vulnerable and unpopular group in an irrational, invidious manner." (*New York Times,* September 28, 1981). In addition to 14th Amendment arguments consideration should be given to the folly of allowing the growth of a resident illiterate untrained youth population which would only add to the public charge for future generations.

POLICY ISSUES FOR AGENCIES

Beyond the myriad of program problems, there are policy issues which arise in relation to services for newcomers. Three such issues will be noted.

There is need for agencies to relate to specific client needs, rather than to try to place newcomers in one of the categorical pigeonholes of the American service system, or use them to fill vacant institutions. A major client problem is to retain ethnic identity, and to have access to natural helping networks during the acculturation process. Placement services which fail to recognize this are not in the best interests of children. A second issue is the need for evenhandedness in programming, regardless of the political and foreign policy issues which brought the client group to the United States in the first place. Agencies cannot justify adjustment of professional standards on the basis of the political popularity of issues associated with the various new arrivals. Finally, with the increasing ethnic composition of our population, spearheaded by the new immigration, it would be helpful if the agency experience with newcomers was more fully integrated into the national delivery system. One approach could be to develop ways in which ethnic associations could interface more effectively with traditional channels for service delivery in both the public and voluntary sectors.

REFERENCES

Citizens' Committee for Children of New York Inc. In Search of Safe Haven, New York, April 1980.

———.Unaccompanied Refugee Minors. New York, April 1981.

Harding, Richard K., and Looney, John G. Problems of Southeast Asian Children in a Refugee Camp. *American Journal of Psychiatry,* April 1977, 134:4, pp. 407-11.

Jenkins, Shirley. The Ethnic Dilemma in Social Services. New York: Free Press, 1981.

Ortiz, Rita. An Experience in Fort McCoy with Unaccompanied Minors. Alumni Newsletter, Columbia University School of Social Work, New York, Fall 1981.

Ramirez, Raul E., and Haney-Gooden, Anne. Undocumented Aliens: A Further Example of the Issues. *Social Work,* Sept. 1979, 24:5, 364.

Salcido, Ramon M. Undocumented Aliens: A study of Mexican Families. *Social Work,* July 1979, 24:4, 306-11.

Intercountry Adoption and Policy Issues

Angela Shen Ryan, MSW

ABSTRACT. With the demand for white babies for adoption greatly exceeding their availability in agencies, adoptive parents have begun to seek children in Asia, South America, and Central America. As a result, intercountry adoption is usually transracial adoption as well. This poses problems similar to those posed by the adoption of native born Black and Hispanic children by white families. Philosophical considerations of intercountry adoption are discussed, pro and con, as are special problems that may be posed in adopting children who may have been traumatized by war, hunger and neglect. The questions of helping Third World countries develop their own social services, and recruiting native born minority families to adopt minority children are addressed. Recommendations are made for developing policy and program around sound intercountry adoption procedures.

Since World War II increasing numbers of children from Asia, South America, and other Third World countries have been adopted by American families. This article, drawing on the author's experience working with the adoption of refugee children from Hong Kong and Korea from 1957 to 1977 as well as the Vietnamese children airlifted here in the mid '70s, will attempt to clarify some of the issues involved in intercountry adoption and to discuss some of their implications for social policy. The subject has particular relevance for human service professionals at a time when increasing numbers of children are confined to refugee camps in Third World countries. In many cases, intercountry adoption is their best hope for a chance in life, and for life itself.

It has been reported that adopted children appear for treatment at psychiatric facilities at a somewhat higher rate than that of children in the general population (Ripple, 1968; Tonssieng, 1962). But

Angela Shen Ryan is a Lecturer at Hunter College School of Social Work, 129 East 79 Street, New York, NY 10021, and City University of New York. She is a Doctoral Student at Fordham University School of Social Work, New York, NY.

because adopted children and their families can be found in all socioeconomic classes, and in cultural, racial, and religious groups all over the country, they are not often considered as members of a cohesive group. Their dispersal has resulted in the lack of sense of group identity or political alliance, so that few interest groups are concerned with their problems. Child welfare professionals are often the only ones left to articulate their needs and draw attention to problems and issues relating to this group.

SCOPE OF INTERCOUNTRY ADOPTION

In the 1940s and '50s, some American couples began to adopt European children. In the late 1960s, a number of Canadian children were placed with American parents. But as these countries began to redevelop their own social services, this source of adoptable children disappeared. During the past ten years, with the demand of white babies for adoption greatly exceeding their availability in agencies, adoptive parents have begun to seek children in other countries. There has been a shift to adopting children from Asia, South America, and Central America. As a result, in most cases intercountry adoption has meant transracial adoption, as well.

From 1966 to 1975 the number of foreign children adopted in the U.S. increased over 400 percent, from 1206 in 1966 to 5672 in 1975 (U.S. Immigration, 1966, 1968, 1974, 1976). Most of the children (30,000) adopted in this period came from Europe and Asia (China, Korea, and Vietnam), but increasing numbers are entering the country from Central and South America. The largest number of adopted children in these years came from Korea (American Public Welfare Assn., 1978).

PHILOSOPHICAL CONSIDERATIONS

Intercountry adoption usually involves adopting children of different race and ethnic background relative to the adoptive family. As a result, this poses problems similar to those posed by the adoption of Black and Hispanic native born children by white families. Those who argue for this type of adoption consider that its humanitarian benefits far outweigh political concerns. Many of these children lack the basic necessities of life. Often they are outcasts of their own societies. Furthermore, many developing countries have no child welfare resources; they simply cannot meet the needs of their homeless children. Intercountry adoption is the best hope these children have for a place to live, be loved, and grow.

Opponents of these adoptions, expressing concern for the child's ethnic and racial identity, sometimes equate transracial adoption with cultural genocide. In 1972, the National Association of Black Social Workers stated their opposition to the placement of black children in white homes for the reason that "Black children in White homes are cut off themselves as Black people, which development is the normal expectation and only true humanistic goal" ("NABSW Opposes . . . "). Other groups such as Native Americans take a similar position; many Indian tribes have taken formal legal action to block off-reservation placement of Indian children (Indian Child Welfare, 1976). It is felt that transracially adopted children are likely to experience identity crises throughout their lives, not accepted by either community. This argument continues around the adoption of Asian children by American white families. When the Vietnamese children were airlifted, there was strong criticism of removing these children from their country of origin. Some critics of intercountry adoption equate the practice with the slave trade of earlier centuries, characterizing it as the ultimate expression of American Imperialism. The outpouring of interest in Vietnamese children was attributed to our "common sense of guilt" (Auerbach, 1975) or "crass political manipulation" (Stearns and Bochnak, 1974).

Questions are often raised as to the propriety of adopting children from other countries when there are many minority children in this country who are in need of adoptive homes (Auerbach, 1975). It is also felt that we could do more to recruit minority families to adopt children of their own race. Some claim that agencies are not preprared to deal with minority adoptive parents and discriminate against them. Offered as evidence is the fact that there are very high rates of informal adoption within the Black community (Katz, 1974) and that there is a high attrition rate among Black couples who do apply to agencies (Ladner, 1977). Language barriers, religious differences, and housing and income eligibility requirements may all combine to discourage the application of immigrant-background parents to adopt children from their own countries of origin.

The question has also been raised as to the placement of refugee children in America as opposed to placement with families in their own countries. In 1974, the U.N. Conference for an International Convention on Adoption Law stressed that whenever possible, a child should be placed in an adoptive home in his/her country of origin. Certainly we should work toward helping Third World countries develop their own child welfare services. There is also much about the adoption process in different cultures that we do not know. For instance, adoption in China is usually a matter of providing a male heir for a family from within the extended family. But studying adoption practices and helping in the development of child welfare services in war-torn and/or economically stricken countries of the Third World will be a long and difficult process. In the meantime there are thousands of children who need homes now. The importance of adoptive families to these orphans engenders concern about the effects of intercountry adoption on these children and families.

EFFECTS OF INTERCOUNTRY ADOPTION ON FAMILIES AND CHILDREN

The desirability and efficacy of transracial and transcultural adoptions have been the subject of many research studies. These studies attempt to observe the child's adjustment in racially mixed families, his racial identity, survival skills, and reaction to cultural factors. Several studies relating to adoption of Black children by white families report success. Grow and Shapiro's study of 125 cases indicated that more than half of these transracial adoptions were successful (1977). Simon and Alton (1977) reported that Black children raised in white families do not acquire ambivalence toward their own race, and that transracial adoption does not jeopardize the non-white child's racial awareness.

Several studies of Korean children placed in American adopting homes suggest successful adjustment despite early problems related to socialization problems, behavior problems, and families' integration into the community (Rosenberg, 1968; Kim, 1978). However, the question of whether white adoptive parents can deal successfully with the racial and cultural identity of children in later years must await further study. Serious research is needed in this area.

In my own experience working with children from China, Korea and Vietnam, I have seen adopted children who come to this country presenting serious health and mental health problems. The following cases will illustrate.

A. Johnny, a 14-year-old boy who came from Hong Kong, was adopted by his own uncle and aunt, who live in a Chinese American community. Though protected by his adoptive parents, Johnny could not cope with the Chinese children who were born here. The adjustment to a pluralistic society, a new language, and a new etiquette resulted in severe depression, that required hospitalization.

B. Judy, a two-year-old Korean, had lived in an orphanage since birth. An adoption was arranged. When she arrived at the airport, we found that at the age of two, she weighed only 15 pounds. Obviously this was an outcast child, maltreated, and suffering from serious malnutrition. She was hospitalized for over a month. Her adoptive parents, shocked by the sight of her at the airport, felt unable to cope with adopting such a child. Eventually another couple was found to adopt her.

C. Charles, age five, was one of the airlifted Vietnamese children. He was placed with an adoptive family five days after his arrival. Because of language difficulties, there was practically no communication between the boy and his adoptive parents. One night he was found in the kitchen with a knife in his hand. A few days later he threatened to jump out the window. With the help of another refugee acting as interpreter, the boy was able to tell about the many violent scenes he had observed in Vietnam. Language difficulties made securing services a problem, but fortunately a Vietnamese psychiatrist was found, and Charles is now in therapy.

These illustrations indicate that adoption of foreign born children, especially from war torn countries, may present significant health and mental health problems. Some of these children may have experienced psychological and physical trauma. Their behavior in adoptive homes must be understood within the context of these experiences as well as the adoption itself, the adoptive family, and the child's developmental needs (Kim, 1980). Often the radical and abrupt disruption of learned routines and the child's reaction to pain and stress may interfere with the bonding process between parents and child. Most families can expect real problems in the enormous emotional and cultural adjustments that accompany intercountry adoption (problems for which, in their excitement at getting a child, the parents may be inadequately prepared). Families need formal and informal supports in meeting these difficulties.

Two mothers whose adopted Korean daughters showed troubled sleep, withdrawn behavior, screaming, hitting, and temper tantrums, wrote:

> We had waited a long time before seeking . . . help because
> our families and friends had reassured us of our ability to cope
> with our problems. Although interested and supportive of our
> efforts, they did not fully understand what we were dealing
> with. Our daughters' experiences were unique and required
> more from us than regular, good parenting ("Infant Adop-
> tion," 1980).

These mothers reported that the interest and suggestions of child
welfare professionals provided them with the encouragement and in-
sights needed to manage their daughters' behavior and regain their
lost confidence.

Not all adoptive applicants have the ability and potential to be
parents of racially and culturally different children. These parents
must be able to understand their child's culture and unique personal
experience. There is also the question of how they will handle the
racism within our society. This author is most concerned about
those parents who reject the fact that Asian and lighter-skinned
children of mixed parentage may face the same discrimination as
Black children. Sometimes adoptive parents will have to examine
their own traces of racism, acknowledge them, and deal with them
in such a way that their children will not be fettered by them (Lien,
1972; Short, 1972).

In most situations, adoptive parents adopt children from other
countries after their experience of not being able to adopt domestically. There is a question of "second-best choice." However, I
have found that parental needs override these reasons and can be used
to overcome whatever prejudice may exist. Humanitarian concerns
for needy children are often a strong motivation. Often the motive
for adopting children of other races and cultures is identical to the
motivation of families who adopt children of the same racial
background: the love for children, and the commitment to having a
family. Adopting a child of another race may be a soul searching experience, requiring working through one's own feelings of racism.
But adoptive families do not see this as unsolvable, even if they experience rejection by friends and families. These parents often
remark that problems are there, but their happiness in receiving
children as their own erases or minimizes all drawbacks.

There remains, of course, the problem of the wider society's
response to an intercountry adoption. No matter how much acceptance white adoptive parents are able to give, adopted children can

obtain the self-esteem for optimal growth only if there is acceptance from the larger community. And foreign adopted children will not escape some hostility. In the 1975 Gallup poll asking whether recently evacuated South Vietnamese should be permitted to live in the United States, the respondents expressed objection by a 52 to 36 percent margin (New Americans . . . ., 1975).

In transracial adoption, adoption agencies should explore with adoptive parents four general areas: (a) racial attitudes; (b) awareness and acceptance of racial/cultural differences; (c) ability to provide support when the child is hurt by racism; and (d) willingness to make a commitment to a lifestyle that will maximize socialization opportunities for the child (Jones and Else, 1979). These same factors can be used as guidelines in evaluating parents' ability to rear a child from another country.

Parents interested in adopting a child from overseas come from all walks of life, and much study is needed to determine which factors relate to success or insuperable difficulties. One research study examining family patterns and adoption, reports that those in the forefront of assuming more contemporary family lifestyles are more amenable to parenting minority children. There appears to be a close affinity between the development of more flexible and interchangeable family roles and the acquisition of wider-ranging perspective of who might be included among family members (Silverman and Feigelman, 1977). The authors' findings suggested that as the trend toward sharing work and child care roles continues, the number of families receptive to the adoption of such children is likely to increase.

The planning of post-adoption services can also be helpful in reducing problems. This author has found that helping these parents contact other parents who can provide supports, share experiences, and give parents a realistic perception of the problems to be faced is most helpful.

PUBLIC POLICY AND INTERCOUNTRY ADOPTION

In general, public policy on intercountry adoption has formed around concern with possible exploitation on an international level. Professional opinion in the early 1970s, when the winding down of the Vietnam War presented the possibility of the arrival of large numbers of Vietnamese children, seriously questioned their adoption (Joe, 1978). The Child Welfare League of America has taken the position that underdeveloped countries should be helped to develop their own child welfare services, rather than placing foreign born children with American parents (Reid, 1975). The United Nations International Children's Emergency Fund does not engage in direct international adoption procedures. UNICEF's concern is to assist nations in establishing services for children within their own countries (United Nations, 1974).

The United States Government has responded to admitting alien children for adoption only through granting individual citizens' petitions or through ad hoc legislation in response to crisis needs, such as passing special legislation to aid refugees displaced by national liberation struggles or socialist revolutions. The Immigration and Naturalization Act of 1965 and the abolition of the National Origin Quota Act have allowed a massive influx of Third World immigrants, but the Immigration and Naturalization Service limits foreign born children to two per adoptive family.

Once a child is placed with the adoptive family, the U.S. Government assumes no legal or financial responsibility. The proposed Family Protection Act, S1378 and H.R. 3955, would provide a tax deduction for adoption expenses—$3500 for domestic adoption and $4500 for international adoption—but the passage of this bill is strongly opposed for other reasons. To date intercountry adoption applicants pay all expenses for the adoption. Naturally this simplifies matters in regard to families with strong financial resources, but difficulties in meeting the costs of adoptions have stymied attempts to widen adoption choices and have led to budget disputes between public and private agencies (Joe, 1978).

Some states have established separately funded intercountry adoption service units. However, there have been problems relating to current procedural notification of the adoption of a child both here and abroad. In some instances, there is no record that placement has occurred, making intervention of problems appear impossible (Meezan, 1980). Only 24 states have statutes referring to foreign country adoptions, and there is considerable variation on special recognition of foreign national adoptions or foreign decree approval. If states do not extend comity to actions taken by foreign nations, the child may be put into a legal "limbo" (American Public Welfare Assn., 1978).

The question of standards has hardly been touched as a matter of public policy. The Child Welfare League of America proposed in

1968 that once adoption in the United States in considered to be in a child's best interest, the same safeguards as for native born children adopted here should apply (1968). Often this standard is not practicable because social services in the child's country of origin are not developed.

Some people view the fragmented and inconsistent status of trans-country regulations as a bonus. An ad hoc approach avoids the kind of visibility which could stampede desperate parents into abandoning children in the hopes of their being rescued by agencies who will see that they reach America (Joe, 1978). However, in some instances, safeguards have delaying features which can harm the waiting child who may be living under emergency conditions and which burden the foreign agency with maintaining the child for a longer period. It is also true that lack of a consistent professional framework leaves children and parents at the mercy of politics and governmental grandstanding. Reacting to severe criticism of intercountry adoption in the mid 1970s, some Third World nations began to institute stringent requirements for both foreign adoptive parents and adoption agencies. Korea reduced the number of adoptive children permitted to go abroad (Matthews, 1977). Columbia, Costa Rica, Ecuador and Nicaragua all instituted a form of moratorium on intercountry adoptions. Procedures were revised to restrict the outward flow of children (Joe, 1978), though there was little follow-through on improving their lot in their own countries. Just recently Brazilian authorities, abruptly and without explanation, barred a group of legally adopted children from leaving Brazil with their American parents ("Brazil blocks . . . ", 1981).

RECOMMENDATIONS

To date, we have not resolved the issue of under what circumstances U.S. citizens or agencies should be allowed to engage in intercountry adoption. As professionals, we need to review the ethics of intercountry adoptions, and then proceed accordingly. It is this author's contention that although other countries should be encouraged to develop their own child welfare services, we cannot just let children, poor, homeless, and suffering from the results of war and violence, live in limbo where existence is subsistance. Intercountry adoption can at least be a transitional method of conveying benefits from those who have to those who have not.

In order to insure that a child is not a victim of our differences it is time to develop sound policy and program around intercountry adoption procedures and practice.

International policy on intercountry adoption is ambiguous, uncoordinated, and unsystematized; this certainly has not been helpful in bringing order to a subject replete with philosophical and practical dilemmas. However, United States agencies could begin examining their own procedures, establishing guidelines and procedures to eliminate obstacles to the placement of American children. State and local program policies relevant to the needs of adoptive children and families should be developed.

Additional recommendations are:

1. The Federal Government must address itself to the task of developing an appropriate policy toward intercountry adoption, including policy relating to immigration and family stability.
2. There is a need to develop an international coordinating agency which could set standards for intercountry adoption. This agency could also help underdeveloped countries set up child welfare services. It could bring "unprofessional placement groups" into conformity with governmental and professional regulations, and survey agencies abroad that operate on agreed upon standards.
3. The Government could help with the costs of intercountry adoption.
4. State Governments should develop statutes regarding foreign country adoptions. All states should have home study provisions; an adoption official within each state should judge the propriety and suitability of a placement.
5. Legal services should be provided to adoptive children and parents.
6. Whenever possible, children should be placed with parents of the same ethnic or racial background.
7. When intercountry adoption involves biracial and bicultural crossings, the decision should be based on the needs of the children as much as possible, rather than the desire of the parents.
8. Parents' motivation for intercountry adoption should be explored carefully. Parents adopting transracially or transculturally must be able to accept differences and incorporate the child's racial and cultural identity.

9. Recognizing the potential for problems, agencies, governmental, or voluntary sources should provide funds and services in post adoptive placement.

10. The Government should provide funding for research in those areas of intercountry adoption that contribute to understanding of racial and cultural identity, personality, · motivational and emotional problems, and processes of the adopted child and the adoptive family.

Despite all the problems, we must not ignore the fact that millions of homeless children populate Third World cities and refugee camps. Over half of the one billion children in the world today lack the basic necessities, most particularly food. America's wealth, and our belief that every child should have the opportunity to grow in an acceptable environment, could be of incalculable worth to the future of these children.

REFERENCES

American Public Welfare Association. *Draft Report of Intercountry Adoptions: Survey of Federal and State Law and Private Sector Policies and Practices.* Washington, D.C.: American Public Welfare Association, April 1978.

Auerbach, Stuart. 120,000 adoptable in U.S., Americans by-passed in rush for Vietnamese. *Washington Post,* April 8, 1975.

Brazil Blocks 13 Adoptions by Americans. *The New York Times,* October 11, 1981, p. 11.

Child Welfare League of America. *Standards for Adoption Services,* Revised Edition. New York: Child Welfare League of America, 1968.

Grow, L., & Shapiro, D. *Black Children—White Families,* New York: Child Welfare League of America, 1977.

Indian Child Welfare: A State of the Field Study. Washington, D. C.: Government Printing Office, 1976 (DHEW: Publication (OHD) 76-30095).

Infant Adoption: Two Family Experiences with Intercountry Adoptions. *Children Today,* November-December 1980, pp. 2-5. The article was written by two mothers whose names have been withheld to protect the privacy of their adopted daughters and their families.

Joe, B. In defense of intercountry adoption. *Social Service Review,* Autumn-March, 1978, pp. 1-20.

Jones, C., & Else. J. Racial and cultural issues in adoption. *Child Welfare,* 1979 *LVIII,* 6, 373-382.

Katz, L.. Transracial adoptions: Some guidelines. *Child Welfare,* 1974, *53*(3) 181.

Kim, Dong Soo. Issues in transracial and transcultural adoption. *Social Casework,* 1978 59 (8) 477-486.

Kim, S. Peter. Behavior symptoms in transracially adopted children: Diagnosis dilemma. *Child Welfare,* 1980, *LIX*(4), 213-224.

Ladner, J. *Mixed families,* Garden City, New York: Anchor Press, 1977.

Lien, M. Letters. *Social Work,* 1972 *17*(5), 109.

Matthews, L. Despite popularity, cute Korean babies aren't for export. *Wall Street Journal,* January 7, 1977.

Meegan, W. *Adoption Service in the States,* U.S. Department of Health and Human Services, Publication No. (OHDS) 80-20388, October 1980.

NABSW Opposes Transracial Adoption, New York: National Association of Black Social Workers, September 1972.

New Americans, Are They Welcome? A Refugee Referendum. *Gallup Opinion Index,* Report No. 119 (May 1975).

Ripple, L. A follow-up study of adopted children. *Social Service Review,* 1968 *42*(4), 479-499.

Rosenberg, A. The adoption of oriental children by Caucasian-American parents. (Master's thesis, University of Wisconsin, 1968).

Short, C. Letters. *Social Work,* 1972 *17*(5), 109-111.

Silverman, A., & Feigelman, W. Some factors affecting the adoption of minority children. *Social Casework, 58*(9), 554-561.

Simon, R., & Alton, H. *Transracial Adoption,* New York: John Wiley and Sons, 1977.

Stearns, M., & Bochnak, E. Indochina Babylift. *Focus on Children and Youth* 1975, *2*(10).

Tonssieng, P. Thoughts regarding the etiology of psychological difficulties in adopted children. *Child Welfare,* 1962, *XLI,* pp. 59-65.

United Nations Economic and Social Council. Protection and welfare of children, report to the Secretary General New York: U.N. Conference for an International Convention on Adoption Law, 1974.

U.S. Immigration and Naturalization Service, *Annual Reports,* fiscal years 1966, 1968, 1974, 1976, Washington, D. C.: Superintendent of Documents, fiscal years, 1966, 1968, 1974, 1976.

EDUCATIONAL ISSUES: BILINGUAL EDUCATION AND RELATED PSYCHOSOCIAL CONCERNS

Language and the Education of Non-English Speaking Children

Katherine Hager Plotnicov, MS

ABSTRACT. This article reviews the issue of language and the education for newcomers and other non-English speaking children in the United States. It portrays fluctuating historical attitudes towards the use of languages, other than English, in schools and other aspects of life, reviews the legal battles on behalf of such children for rights to equal educational opportunities, describes arguments favoring and opposing bilingual education, and depicts current federal policy regarding the educational rights of these children.

The issue of language of instruction for immigrant children has surfaced periodically in the history of our country, and recently with steadily increasing numbers of newcomer children entering the nation's schools, it has again become salient. A 1975 survey of the Census Bureau reported over three million children with no or limited English-speaking (NES/LES) ability in the nation's schools

Katherine Hager Plotnicov has a degree in Child Development and Child Care, and is a Graduate Student in the Doctoral Program of Educational Psychology, University of Pittsburgh, PA 15260.

(Rosenbaum, 1981). Our country's schools are confronted with a major problem: how to meet the language needs of these children. The issue is of crucial importance to the successful adaptation of these children for whom a lack of proficiency in English has been viewed not just as a major deterrent to school achievement (Alexander, Mountjoy, & Sjorgen, 1920), but also ultimately to the social mobility for the individual or ethnic group (Paulston, 1978).

Numerous factors, however, preclude the possibility of a single or simple solution. Among these factors are, first of all, the diverse characteristics of the newcomers themselves, such as different cultural and linguistic backgrounds, geographical dispersion upon resettlement, dissimilar intentions regarding settling permanently or returning, different entry status and entitlements, and the presence or absence of a pre-established ethnic community. There is also the cumbersome structure of our legal system and the diverse characteristics of autonomously functioning local school districts with differing constituencies, limited funds and human resources. The result has been a mixed response to the language needs of these children, ranging from inadequate provision to elaborate programs of bilingual/bicultural education. Proponents of different approaches argue heatedly over the merits of favored programs, particularly bilingual education. This paper provides a brief overview of the issue of schools' responses to the language needs of newcomer children. It reviews the history of change in attitudes toward the use of languages other than English in the United States, describes the legal battles of these children for equal education, reports the current federal policy toward the language needs of these children, and reviews arguments around the issue of bilingual education.

ATTITUDES REGARDING THE USE
OF FOREIGN LANGUAGES

An historical review of attitudes towards the use of languages, other than English, in this country reveals wide fluctuations in trends from open acceptance to virtual prohibition. Settled by immigrants who spoke many different native tongues, America has never had an official national language, although English has been the traditional language of government. In America's beginnings, it was common for immigrants to use their native language among themselves and, in areas with heavy concentrations of settlers sharing a common language, that language was sometimes spoken in the business of local government, in the lower courts, and in the schools. Immigrants typically realized it to be in their best interests to learn English, and there was little effort on the part of the national government during the nineteenth century to discourage the use of other languages. The major exception to this policy was not toward the immigrants, but rather toward those indigenous or early-established groups whose cultural and linguistic differences were considered a threat to national unity—namely, the American Indians, the French speakers of Louisiana, and the Spanish speakers of New Mexico (Ridge, 1981; Wagner, 1981).

During the late 1800s, strong anti-foreign sentiment developed and became expressed in movements to restrict immigration and in the passage of laws in several states to eliminate general instruction in languages other than English. This trend intensified in the beginning of this century and was promoted by such prominent political figures as Theodore Roosevelt, who advocated the philosophy of "America for Americans." In 1906, English speaking ability became a requirement for naturalization. Xenophobic sentiment peaked during the first World War and was accompanied by the passage of local and state laws prohibiting the instruction in schools of foreign languages, particularly German. (These laws were later overturned by the Supreme Court.) Restrictive quota systems reduced the numbers of new, non-English speaking arrivals. The expectation was for immigrants to become assimilated and acculturated as rapidly as possible which, of course, demanded their acquisition of the English language. Immigrant children were immersed in regular classrooms, whose job it was to Americanize them. Indeed, most immigrants were themselves eager to accept the ways of their new country. Those who wished to maintain their native language and culture did so on their own, as exemplified by the after-school Hebrew schools or the Japanese Saturday schools in California. The principal exceptions to the English-speaking rule were the long established Hispanic communities in New Mexico and the protectorate of Puerto Rico, where Spanish remained dominant (Glazer, 1981; Nunis, 1981; Rosenbaum, 1981; Wagner, 1981).

Anti-foreign sentiment gradually abated. Large numbers of Eastern European refugees were admitted after the second World War, and the immigration quota systems based on selection by national origin were weakened. The trend toward greater acceptance of cultural and concurrently, linguistic diversity continued to grow, and by the 1960s, along with increased concern for civil rights, came movements built around pride in ethnic heritage, beginning among Black Americans and diffusing to other ethnic minorities, such as Native Americans, Hispanic Americans, and others. The outgrowth of this ideological development was the enactment of laws asserting the rights of all children with limited or no proficiency in the English language to participate equally in the educational process and specifically promoting bilingual education, both as a means to this end and for the maintenance of native culture and language (Rosenbaum, 1981; Wagner, 1981).

LEGAL RESPONSES TO THE EDUCATIONAL NEEDS OF NES/LES CHILDREN

The legal history of the right of children with no or limited English proficiency to special (ESL, Bilingual etc.) educational programs, which began in the 1960s, has during the two intervening decades experienced a course marked by rapid gains followed by substantial setbacks. While the right of such children to special educational programs has become established, the language of the law has left open the question of what may constitute these programs; bilingual education, or simply programs to develop proficiency in English. It has been the job of the courts to respond to this question. The course of these legal developments along with a description of Department of Education and Office of Civil Rights policy at the time of this writing are outlined below.

The Bilingual Education Act of 1968 was the first major piece of legislation addressing the educational needs of NES/LES children. It developed out of the recognition that large numbers of children with a dominance in other languages, particularly Spanish, were unable to benefit from their schooling because of English language deficiency. This act was designed to remedy such deficiencies by encouraging schools to provide transitional bilingual instruction, with federal funding for bilingual programs as the incentive. Their implementation was, however, entirely voluntary on the part of school districts (Rosenbaum, 1981; Wagner, 1981).

Subsequent federal efforts to address the educational needs of these children—a group which has greatly expanded to encompass all the recent immigrants, refugees and undocumented aliens, as well as the previously established ethnic enclaves—have taken a firmer approach based on sanctions for noncompliance rather than rewards. These efforts have been based primarily on civil rights legislation (the Civil Rights Act of 1964, Title VI [henceforth referred to as Title VI]), which bans discriminatory practices in programs receiving federal assistance. While these measures clearly assert the right of NES/LES children to special educational programs, they do not take a clear and consistent position on the issue of bilingual education.

In May of 1970, a memorandum was circulated by the Director of the Office of Civil Rights (O.C.R.), J. Stanley Pottinger, to school districts with enrollments of greater than 5 percent national origin-minority group children that delineated the responsibility of school districts to comply with Title VI by opening instructional programs to children whose limited English proficiency hindered their effective participation. This document required school districts to "take affirmative steps to rectify the language deficiency" of these children; it prohibited their placement in classes for the mentally retarded on the basis of language skills; it demanded that remedial measures be implemented soon after such children were classified, and it required that notification of activities be made to parents in a language understandable to them. This memorandum did not prescribe the nature of such "affirmative steps."

The major boost to the cause of bilingual education followed the *Lau v. Nichols* (1974) Supreme Court decision. This case was brought on behalf of 1,800 Chinese-speaking children against the San Francisco public school system which had failed to provide them supplemental instruction in English. Basing its position on Title VI, the Court, in keeping with the 1970 HEW guidelines, ruled that the schools needed to provide a program to meet the language needs of the plaintiffs. However it did not stipulate what those remedies must be. The Court determined it to be the duty of the O.C.R. to interpret and enforce a school's compliance with Title VI. An O.C.R. task force then published advisory guidelines for compliance to Title VI, the "*Lau* Remedies." The *Lau* Remedies strongly emphasized the use of bilingual approaches for children with no English proficiency, both Transitional Bilingual Education (TBE) and Bilingual/Bicultural or Multilingual/Multicultural Programs (BBP, MMP). While English as a Second Language (ESL) was to be part of all programs, only at the high school level were programs based exclusively on this approach deemed acceptable. School districts were not compelled to adopt the *Lau* recommendations, but those that could not demonstrate their own programs to be equally effective risked the withdrawal of federal funds.

In the same year, Congress "codified the essence of *Lau*" by the passage of the Equal Educational Opportunities Act of 1974 (EEOA) which required schools to take appropriate action to effectively open participation in instruction to students with deficiencies in English (Rosenbaum, 1981). However, the language of this Act, as with *Lau*, avoided defining "appropriate action," and so, whether such remedies meant the right to bilingual education reverted to the courts to determine. In the time immediately following *Lau*, courts looked favorably on bilingual education (as in *Serna, Aspira,* and *Keys* [Steinman, 1975]). The strong influence of *Lau* was also felt in the implementation of some sort of bilingual program in 22 states (Rosenbaum, 1981). Similarly, the administration under President Carter sought to solidify the gains of *Lau* by proposing rules which defined bilingual programs as the standard for compliance to Title VI (Wagner, 1981; Rosenbaum, 1981).

Judicial and administrative support for bilingual programs has weakened with the change in administration. Perhaps this reflects the interaction of factors such as a depressed economy and unfavorable public reactions to the large influx of Cuban and Haitian refugees. The Department of Education proposals were withdrawn. President Reagan has himself denounced bilingual education as creating an "economic handicap" for national origin-minority group children (Rosenbaum, 1981; Wagner, 1981). Under the present Secretary of Education, T. H. Bell, *Lau* guidelines are no longer considered the standard for measuring Title VI compliance. Current policy, instead of favoring a bilingual approach, emphasizes "flexibility" in school districts' responses to the needs of children with limited English proficiency. The Department of Education now requires that the following conditions be met. First, the memorandum of May 1970 (described above) is still observed. School districts must identify children for whom English is not the dominant language, assess their proficiency in English, and provide a program to meet their educational needs. This program need not be bilingual. Standards for such programs are now based on the U. S. Court of Appeals Fifth Circuit decision in *Casteneda v. Pickard* (1981) which requires: (a) that the program is based on "sound educational theory" endorsed by "some experts in the field"; (b) that it is reasonably implemented; and (c) that there are provisions for evaluating whether its intended effects are being realized. Efforts to enforce these policies consist of routine monitoring and investigating by O.C.R. as well as complaint review investigations. Under present procedures, when noncompliance is found, school districts may enter into negotiations with the O.C.R. to reconcile their differences and then submit a compliance plan. The ultimate sanction for noncompliance remains the withdrawal of federal funds.

DEFENSES AND CRITICISMS
OF THE BILINGUAL APPROACH

It is apparent from the above description of the recent legal history of bilingual education that there are powerful political forces and strong arguments on all sides of the issue. Are bilingual programs best suited to the needs of these children, or are methods based exclusively on establishing English proficiency equally appropriate? Some of the major positions and their rationales are summarized here.

Among the most outspoken proponents of bilingual education are those minority groups who see it as a means of preserving native language and culture. They argue that bilingual/bicultural education enhances children's self-esteem and promotes respect for cultures other than that of white, middle class America. They see it also as an avenue toward the achievement of social justice and equality by opening educational opportunity to their children. Such programs provide jobs for ethnic minority group members. Bilingual/bicultural education acknowledges the right of ethnic groups to remain distinct; it supports cultural pluralism. In some cases, as with migrant laborers, knowledge of native language and culture are also of paramount pragmatic importance in facilitating adjustment when families return to their homeland (Glazer, 1981; Laosa, 1974; Nunis, 1981; Paulston, 1978; Ridge, 1981; Rosenbaum, 1981).

Others favor bilingual education primarily because of its believed educational effectiveness. They contend that development of the mother tongue enhances concept development and facilitates second language acquisition; they argue further that if the first language is inadequately developed, the result may be poor development in both languages, a condition known as semilingualism (Paulston, 1978). Others do not see bilingual education as an end in itself, but view it as transitional in nature, serving as a bridge into full participation in the mainstream. Native language instruction in academic subjects, along with training in English, permits students to stay on grade level until development of English skills permits their understanding in regular classes (Carlucci, 1974).

Opponents of bilingual education hold that cultural and linguistic maintenance are private matters, a position for which there is strong precedent in the history of many ethnic groups in this country who have sent their children to full-time, part-time, or weekend private or parochial, ethnic or religious schools (Nunis, 1981; Rosenbaum, 1981). Furthermore, they argue that differences in the customs and language of a single ethnic group would result in disagreement over which dialect or which custom to teach (as with the Jews or the Spanish-speakers from all of Central and South America). They contend that historically, bilingual education was not necessary to the superior achievement of certain ethnic groups, nor is it today. They also challenge the effectiveness of bilingual education. Some argue that bilingual/bicultural instruction creates a source of political divisiveness, fostering foreign loyalties. Perhaps the simplest and most compelling argument is that many school districts lack the financial and human resources (such as teachers fluent in Vietnamese, Thai, Portuguese, etc.) to implement bilingual programs for their students (Glazer, 1981; Thompson, 1980).

CONCLUSION

The issue of language of instruction for children with limited English proficiency is both complex and controversial. Differences exist both with respect to the ends and the means in the education of these children. Should the goal in public education be the maintenance of native language and culture, or simply the elimination of deficiencies in English and other discriminatory practices which limit their full participation in the educational process? If the goal is the former, then the means are clearly bilingual/bicultural programs. If the goal is the latter, however, the choice of alternative means is broad, with bilingual education constituting one of many options. As Under-Secretary Carlucci observed in 1974, no single choice is appropriate in all instances. Rather, the choice must depend on numerous considerations, such as the concentration of students with limited English proficiency within a particular school district, the number of different languages spoken, children's degree of proficiency in English, and their ages. It may well represent the choice of many state and local educational agencies, in consideration of large numbers of national origin-minority group children, to institute various types of bilingual programs. However, at the level of federal law and policy, the goal at present is more circumspect—namely, to address the language deficiencies by any educationally sound and effective means in keeping with civil rights. While this position represents at least a temporary setback to the cause of bilingual education, its effects on the educational opportunities of newcomers and other LES/NES children cannot yet be assessed. On the one hand, a policy of increased flexibility may avoid the bureaucratic rigidity which requires treating "all alike when they are not" (Glazer, 1981). It may permit local educational agencies to respond more appropriately to the needs of their particular student body, and it may enhance experimentation. On the other hand, such "flexibility" may mask a policy of benign neglect, where loopholes abound for those who seek to abide by the letter but not the spirit of the law.

REFERENCES

Alexander, F. Q., Mountjoy, B. M., and Sjorgen, C. Foreign students in the U. S.: New help for high schools. *The College Board Review,* 1980, 2-7.

Carlucci, F. Memorandum DHEW, December 2, 1974. (ERIC Document Reproduction Service No. ED 158 358).

Casteneda v. Pickard. Federal Reporter, 2nd Series, 1981, *648,* 989.

Glazer, N. Pluralism and the new immigrants. *Society,* 1981, *19*(1), 31-36.

Laosa, L. Child care and the culturally different child. *Child Care Quarterly,* 1974, 3(4), 214-224.

Lau v. Nichols, United States Reporter, 1974, *414,* 563.

Nunis, D. B. Jr. American identities. *Society,* 1981, *19*(1), 29-30.

Paulston, C. B. Linguistic aspects of emigrant children (ERIC Document Reproduction Service No. ED 144 340).

Pottinger, J. S. Memorandum of May 25, 1970. Identification of discrimination and denial of services on the basis of national origin. (ERIC Document Reproduction Service No. ED 158 358). Also, 35 Fed. Reg. 11595.

Ridge, M. Multiple loyalties: An American dilemma. *Society,* 1981, *19*(1), 59-62.

Rosenbaum, S. Educating children of immigrant workers: Language policies in France and the U. S. A. *American Journal of Comparative Law,* 1981, *29,* 429-465.

Steinman, E. H. The *Lau v. Nichols* Supreme Court Decision of 1974. Testimony of E. H. Steinman before the Committee on Ways and Means of the California State Assembly. Catesol Occasional Papers, 1975, No. 2 (ERIC Document Reproduction Service No. ED 116 457).

Task Force Findings Specifying Remedies Available for Eliminating Past Educational Practices Ruled Unlawful under *Lau v. Nichols.* Office of Civil Rights (ERIC Document Reproduction Service No. 158 358).

Thompson, M. How schools are helping kids who can't speak English. *The American School Board Journal,* 1980, *167,* 35-39.

Wagner, S. T. America's non-English heritage. *Society,* 1981, *19*(1), 37-44.

Self-Concept, English Language Acquisition, and School Adaptation in Recently Immigrated Asian Children

S. Peter Kim, MD

ABSTRACT. This paper reports the results of a preliminary study of 12 native Korean immigrant children, between the ages of 7 1/2 and 10 years, who had lived in the United States for less than a year at the time of the first study evaluation. The purpose of the study was to evaluate the relationship among the level of self-concept, the pattern of English language acquisition (rapidity and proficiency), and school adaptation and achievement.

Since the 1965 Immigration and Naturalization Act Amendments that virtually eliminated the restrictive national origin quota system in issuing immigration visas to the United States, the number of immigrants from the east and southeast Asian countries sharply increased. While 16,300 immigrants arrived from east Asia in 1965, the number increased to 103,800 in 1975. The total number of newcomers from the same region between 1965 and 1975 was 753,302 (U.S. Immigration and Naturalization Service Annual Reports). Approximately one-third of these Asian immigrants (240,000) were of school age (under 19 years of age), and still more are to come to this country. The number of Korean immigrants increased by 1,300 percent between 1965 and 1975, ranking them numerically second only to the Filipino immigrants among Asian groups.

Dr. Kim is Associate Professor of Psychiatry and Director of Training and Education, Division of Child and Adolescent Psychiatry, in the Department of Psychiatry, New York University Medical Center, 550 First Avenue, New York, NY 10016.

This investigation was supported by N.I.M.H. Grant No. 5-T01-MH13455, Psychiatry G.P. Special Training.

Many adjustmental and adaptive difficulties arise when immigrant families move into a society of a totally alien culture with a heritage of traditional values. Children of these families have to carry dual burdens of having to achieve their age-appropriate developmental tasks as well as having to go through the process of acculturation and transcultural adjustment in the new society. Very little is known about the various developmental and adjustmental aspects of these Asian immigrant children, and few studies have been done in these areas (Hakuta and Cancino, 1977). A few basic sociological study reports on these families and children are beginning to emerge.

The purpose of the present study is to investigate the correlation between the transcultural child's self-concept, patterns (rapidity and proficiency) of English language acquisition, and school adaptation and achievement. The study was designed to test the following hypotheses: Given similar intelligence (1) children with a high self-concept learn English faster and better than those with a low self-concept; (2) children with a high self-concept adapt better to their new school environment and show better school performance; (3) there is a positive correlation between language proficiency in English and the degree of school adaptation and achievement; (4) children whose parents consciously attempted to help them retain the original language (Korean) have a high self-concept.

METHODS

Subjects

The study subjects consisted of 12 native Korean children, between the ages 7 1/2 and 10 years (second through fifth grades), randomly selected regardless of sex from the Greater New York area, who had lived in the United States less than one year and had attended school less than six months at the time of the initial evaluation. The children with developmental disorders (mental retardation and childhood psychosis), genetic disorders, chronic physical illness, physical anomalies or handicaps, special sensory organ disorders, visual-motor perceptual disorders and known learning disorders were excluded from the study. Twins were also excluded. Only children with an intelligence quotient above 100 were included in the study.

Evaluations and Assessment Instruments

A. Family Assessments

Parents were interviewed to gather information regarding family history, demographic data including socioeconomic status, child's birth and past illness history, developmental and school history.

B. Child Evaluation

Initial Intelligence Assessment for Clinical Estimation of I.Q. was done by use of selected subtest items from the Wechsler Intelligence Scale for Children (WISC-R), the Draw-A-Person Test, and the Wide Range Achievement Test. These tests were administered bilingually and items were translated into Korean if necessary. Also, a *Standard Mental Status Examination* was done on each child.

The following questionnaires and assessments were given to each study child at the child's initial evaluation and again six months later:

1. *Piers-Harris (P-H) Children's Self-Concept Scale ("The Way I Feel About Myself")* (Piers, 1969, 1976), consisting of 80 standardized question items. The responses are classified into six factor categories (I. Behavior; II. Intellectual and School Status; III. Physical Appearance and Attributes; IV. Anxiety; V. Popularity; VI. Happiness and Satisfaction).

Each child's raw score (range 10-80) was converted into percentile according to the conversion table. Then the percentile was classified into a 3-point weighted score: 3 for those above 60% (high self-concept group); 2 for 40-60% (average self-concept group); 1 for below 40% (low self-concept group).

2. *Language Proficiency Assessment* in English consisting of three major categories, namely, *articulatory, semantic,* and *syntactic.* Each category is rated on a weighted score of 1 to 3. The test texts are from the readers of elementary school grades 2-5 in Korean and English.

3. *School Adaptation and Achievement Inventory* consisting of two sub-areas, namely, *academic performance* and *school social-personal competence.* Each sub-area has ten items to be rated in weighted scores of 1 to 3. The inventory items are completed by the child's school teacher (Table 1).

Table 1

School Adaptation and Achievement Inventory

(Weighted Scores: 3 = High; 2 = Average; 1 = Low)

Academic Performance	Score
(circle one)	
1. Reading (grade-appropriate level)	3 2 1
2. Writing (grade-appropriate level)	3 2 1
3. Arithmetic (grade-appropriate level)	3 2 1
4. Always attentive in classroom	3 2 1
5. Likes and looks forward to school	3 2 1
6. Always finishes school work and homework on time	3 2 1
7. Actively participates in classes	3 2 1
8. Readily asks questions and corrects own mistakes	3 2 1
9. Always works hard to learn and improve	3 2 1
10. Other (e.g., arts, sports, etc.) (Specify:)	3 2 1
Average Score (I):	_____

School Social-Personal Competence	Score
1. Actively approaches peers	3 2 1
2. Expresses self well to others	3 2 1
3. Has many friends	3 2 1
4. Often volunteers in school	3 2 1
5. Likes and actively participates in sports and games	3 2 1
6. Readily admits own faults and mistakes	3 2 1
7. Readily appreciates others' merits	3 2 1
8. Conscientious, trustworthy and responsible	3 2 1
9. Always in positive mood, affable and friendly	3 2 1
10. Other (Specify:)	3 2 1
Average Score (II):	

Overall Average Score = $\frac{(I) + (II)}{2}$ = ☐

RESULTS

The family data from parental interview and the initial and second evaluation findings of each child were tabulated (Table 2), and statistical analyses of results indicated the following:

1. The families of the study children are classified into socioeconomic status class II-III (Hollingshead & Redlich, 1958).

2. The children in the high and average self-concept groups showed significantly higher language proficiency progress scores compared to the children in the low self-concept group. There were no significant differences in language proficiency progress scores between the high and average self-concept groups. These findings confirm the first study hypothesis (Table 3).

3. The children in the high self-concept group showed significantly higher school acheivement and adaptation (SAA) progress scores compared to the children in the average and low self-concept group. There were no significant differences in the SAA progress scores among the average and the low self-concept groups. These findings confirm the second study hypothesis (Table 4).

4. The children in the high language proficiency (LP) group showed significantly higher second SAA scores compared to those of children in the low LP group, confirming the third study hypothesis (Table 5).

5. All the parents of the study children attempted consciously, although the extent of efforts varied, to help their children retain the original language (Korean). Therefore the fourth study hypothesis could not be tested.

Table 2

Subjects			P-H Scale Scores*				Language Proficiency**		School Achievement & Adaptation***	
			Percentile & Weighted Score				Overall Average Weight. Scores		Overall Average Weight. Scores	
			Initial		Second					
No.	Sex	(Initial)	%	W.S.	%	W.S.	Initial	Second	Initial	Second
1	M	7-2	71	3	74	3	1.67	3.00	1.6	2.8
2	M	7-8	96	3	96	3	2.00	3.00	2.0	2.9
3	M	8-4	52	2	57	2	1.33	2.67	1.8	2.6
4	F	7-9	98	3	98	3	1.33	3.00	1.4	3.0
5	F	8-6	33	1	36	1	1.00	1.33	1.2	1.8
6	M	9-2	94	3	93	3	1.00	3.00	1.6	3.0
7	M	9-8	49	2	52	2	1.00	2.67	1.6	2.4
8	F	9-0	38	1	44	2	1.00	2.00	1.2	2.0
9	F	9-8	87	3	93	3	1.33	3.00	1.5	2.9
10	M	10-2	55	2	57	2	1.00	2.33	1.6	2.6
11	M	9-3	36	1	41	2	1.00	1.67	1.0	1.5
12	F	9-6	38	1	38	1	1.00	1.33	1.3	2.0

* (t = 0.501, df = 22, p < 0.6)
** (t = 16.926, df = 22, p < 0.01)
*** (t = 5.769, df = 22, p < 0.01)

Table 3

English Language Acquisition Progress
Compared Among Three P-H Scale Score Subgroups

Language Proficiency (LP) Progress

(difference between first and second
Overall Average Weighted Scores)

Group I		Group II		Group III	
Subjects with High P-H Weighted Scores		Subjects with Average P-H Weighted Scores		Subjects with Low P-H Weighted Scores	
Subject Number	LP Score Difference	Subject Number	LP Score Difference	Subject Number	LP Score Difference
1	1.33	3	1.34	5	0.33
2	1.00	7	1.67	8	1.00
4	1.67	10	1.33	11	0.67
6	2.00			12	0.33
9	1.67				
(N = 5)		(N = 3)		(N = 4)	

Group I vs. Group III: t = 3.979, df = 7, p<0.01
Group II vs. Group III: t = 4.08, df = 5, p<0.01
Group I vs. Group II: t = 0.361, df = 6, p<0.7 (N.S.)

Table 4

School Adaptation and Achievement (SAA) Progress* Compared Among Three P-H Scale Score Subgroups

Group I — Subjects with High P-H Weighted Scores		Group II — Subjects with Average P-H Weighted Scores		Group III — Subjects with Low P-H Weighted Scores	
Subject Number	SAA Progress	Subject Number	SAA Progress	Subject Number	SAA Progress
1	1.2	3	0.8	5	0.6
2	0.9	7	0.8	8	0.8
4	1.6	10	1.0	11	0.5
6	1.4			12	0.7
9	1.4				
(N = 5)		(N = 3)		(N = 4)	

*The difference between the first and the second overall average SAA weighted scores of a study child

Group I vs. Group III: $t = 4.483$, df = 7, $p < 0.01$
Group II vs. Group III: $t = 2.309$, df = 5, $p < 0.07$ (N.S.)
Group I vs. Group II: $t = 2.624$, df = 6, $p < 0.05$

Table 5

Language Proficiency (LP) Versus
School Adaptation and Achievement (SAA)

High Proficiency Group
(Second LP Score > 2.00)

Subject Number	Second SAA Score
1	2.8
2	2.9
3	2.6
4	3.0
6	3.0
7	2.4
9	2.9
10	2.6

(N = 8)

Low Proficiency Group
(Second LP Score ≤ 2.00)

Subject Number	Second SAA Score
5	1.8
8	2.0
11	1.5
12	2.0

(N = 4)

(N = 8)

($t = 6.934$, $df = 10$, $p < 0.01$)

DISCUSSION

With the recent significant increase in the number of Asian immigrants settling in this country, demands for various educational, social, and health services for this new minority group have increased in both private and public sectors. The present dearth of knowledge available to professionals (especially those in education and child/youth mental health) seeking to assist the Asian immigrant child's adaptation and settlement in the United States makes further systematic studies relevant and urgent.

Results of this preliminary study of 12 Korean children indicate that there is a significant, positive correlationship between the three variables: level of self-concept, degree of linguistic proficiency, and school adaptation and achievement. None of the subjects in this study manifested signs of behavior disorders.

The study results warrant a further longitudinal study of a large population of Asian minority children to elucidate the patterns of adjustment and the later incidence and mechanisms of behavior disorder development. Until these data are compiled, analyzed, and validated for clinical application, the rendering of optimal psychosocioeducational services for these minority children cannot be realized.

REFERENCES

Hakuta, K., & Cancino, H. Trends in second-language acquisition research. *Harvard Educational Review,* 1977, 47(3); 294-316.

Hollingshead, A. B., & Redlich, F. C. *Social Class and Mental Illness.* New York: John Wiley & Sons, 1958.

Piers, E. V. *Manual for the Piers-Harris Children's Self Concept Scale (The Way I Feel About Myself).* Nashville: Counselor Recordings and Tests, 1969.

Piers, E. V. *The Piers-Harris Children's Self Concept Scale: Research Monograph #1.* Nashville: Counselor Recordings and Tests, 1976.

U.S. Immigration and Naturalization Service *Annual Reports,* Fiscal Years 1966-1976, Washington, D.C.

Problems in the Delivery of the School Based Psycho-Educational Services to the Asian Immigrant Children

Yang J. Kim, PhD

ABSTRACT. Despite the many and varied psycho-educational needs of Asian immigrant children in public schools, these children seldom come to the attention of the school based support team (SBST) for its psychological, educational, and/or social work intervention. Problems existing in the delivery of these services to Asian immigrant children are examined in the context of: 1) referral inhibiting characteristics of the children; 2) stereotype-inspired expectations of the teachers; and 3) referral discouraging educational policies. Invisibility of the children, expectations of passivity by the teachers, inadequate educational policies, and limited availability of qualified bilingual and bicultural staff are discussed. Recommendations are made to improve current situations plagued with problems.

In response to the Public Law 94-142: *The Education of All Handicapped Act of 1975* which mandates provision of multidisciplinary support services to children who need psychological, educational, and/or social work services to ameliorate particular handicapping conditions(s) which interfere with their optimal growth and development in school setting, the School Based Support Team (SBST) has been operating in the New York City public schools since September of 1980. The Team, consisting of a school psychologist, a school social worker, and an educational evaluator, interviews children, parents and school personnel regarding the children's needs; administers psychological and/or educational tests; provides counseling services; and makes recommendations for special educational

Yang J. Kim is a school psychologist with the New York City Public Schools, New York, NY.

81

programs and/or placement for those who can benefit from such arrangements.

Considering the multiple handicapping situations associated with immigration from Asia to this vastly different cultural milieu which face the fresh-off-the-plane immigrant children, one would expect that these children as a group would constitute a bulk of referral to SBST. However, the existing statistics defy logical expectations. A quick survey of the referral on Asian immigrant children to various Committees on the Handicapped offices in New York City school subdivisions indicates that these children rarely come to the attention of the School Based Support Teams. The author, having been working with the New York City public school system in Manhattan areas for the past eight years, has received only seven referrals on Asian immigrant children of Korean origin, consisting of one case of hard-of-hearing, 1 case of mental retardation associated with congenital developmental disorders, 1 speech and language disability, 3 emotional disturbances, and 1 case of delinquency. Considering that approximately 15,000 Korean immigrants have settled in this area, this number seems to be strikingly low. A similar situation has been reported in Flushing, Queens, where approximately 20,000 new Korean immigrants reside. Except for the problem of language barrier, these children do appear immune to "problems," according to the Committee on The Handicapped in this area. Low rates of referral have been reported for the Filipino, Chinese and Asian-Indian groups.

In the Korean cases, the children referred have been found to suffer from severe handicapping conditions of physical and/or medical nature or from moderate to extreme cases of emotional and/or behavioral disturbances, all of which required immediate, "Special Education" placement. The severity of the conditions in these referrals was much more obvious and unmistakable. This phenomenon has been observed in working with other Asian groups (Bourne, 1975). An experienced guidance coordinator in a New York City school district serving a large Chinese-American child population once mentioned, "The Chinese kids are either very good or very bad. The bad ones are really crazy. Thank God, there aren't that many bad ones."

Where are the Asian immigrant children? Fresh from planes and boats, are they problem-free and functioning well in school? The conspicuously low rate of referrals on Asian immigrant children can be examined in the following contexts:

1. Referral inhibiting characteristics of the children,
2. Stereotype-inspired expectations of the teachers; and,
3. Referral discouraging educational policies.

REFERRAL INHIBITING CHARACTERISTICS OF THE CHILDREN

Despite the widely held notion by the majority of Americans that Asian and Asian-American children in this country have few psychological and/or educational problems and are functioning effectively in school, a host of psycho-educational problems have been noted in recent literature, including heightened anxiety and loneliness (Sue & Kirk, 1972); low self ratings on perceived popularity (Chang, 1975); low verbal achievement scores (Chu, 1971); introversion, anxiety, neuroticism, and low leadership potential (Meredith, 1966).

These problems, however, have been kept unnoticed in classroom situations to the extent that these children are largely invisible in school settings (Kuroiwa, 1975). Handicapped by their language barrier and culture shock, these children tend to resort to passivity and conformity, taking an invisible role in a school which rewards the assertive and highly verbal behavior.

Passivity and conformity have profound implications for educational, social and emotional development of school children. Active (and/or non-conforming) children usually manage to capture the attention of their teacher. Their frequent verbalizations of likes and dislikes, their assertive stance in insisting on rights and opinions, their independent and challenging approach to the classroom situations, and their tendency to lead or stir up the group keep them clearly audible and visible. Passive (and/or conforming) children, on the other hand, seldom manage to receive their share of attention from the teacher. Their quietness, inconspicuousness, withdrawal, and non-threatening stance in the classroom tend to make them less noticeable. A teacher might not recognize a certain behavioral manifestation of passivity as a sign of poor adjustment, and even if she/he does, it is probable that she/he considers it less serious in nature.

Aversion toward assertion and antipathy for articulation in a student of Asian descent were considered as major contributing factors to the findings of the studies at the University of California,

Berkeley, which revealed that an Asian-American student is twice as likely to fail the Subject A examination, a test of English proficiency, as his non-Asian classmates. Out of a random sample of 300 Asian-American students, 53% failed to demonstrate competence in college level reading and composition as compared to 25% of the general population. A study of majors chosen by Asian-American students shows that during the period from 1961 to 1968, 74.3% of Chinese-American and 68.2% of Japanese-American males went into either engineering or physical sciences, disciplines requiring a minimum of self-expression (Watanabe, 1973).

STEREOTYPE-INSPIRED EXPECTATIONS OF THE TEACHERS

Kim (1980) found that race stereotyping of Asian-American children exists among elementary school teachers along the activity/passivity dimension. Teachers tend to perceive passive Asian-American children as being better adjusted to the classroom as compared to passive Caucasian children. Also, the teachers tend to perceive active Asian-American children as being less well adjusted to the classroom as compared to active Caucasian children. Thus, the teachers perceive the same degree of activity and passivity in an Asian and in a non-Asian child differently in terms of severity of adjustment problem in the classroom setting.

In view of the remarkably low referral rates of the Asian immigrant children for psycho-educational intervention, the stereotype-inspired expectation of passivity in these children should be given critical examination. For instance, a five-year-old, Asian immigrant child may come to school behaving in a non-expressive, non-assertive, dependent, and inhibited manner. She/he may be extremely shy, ask no questions, volunteer no answers and be easily intimidated by aggressive peers. If the teacher believes that this is a "typical" Asian-American child, behaving as expected, or the teacher dismisses the child's behavior as something that the child will grow out of as she/he develops English proficiency, the teacher is likely to give the child little attention and the child is bound to miss the opportunity to be taught more adaptable modes of behavior at this early stage of development when behavior can be modified. There is abundant evidence which indicates that expectations of others can affect behavior as self-fulfilling prophesy (Deutsch & Collins, 1952; Palardy, 1969; Rothenthal & Jacobson, 1968).

Racial stereotyping pervades school environment. It has been shown that children's books on Asians and Asian-Americans currently in print or in use in schools and libraries portray these people in a distinctly stereotyped manner. A comprehensive analysis of 66 books published between 1945 and 1975, in which one or more central characters were Asian or Asian-American revealed that these books contained "loaded" words, images and situations which suggested that these people are passive, docile, unquestioning, obedient, reserved, serene, quiet, exceedingly accommodating, and the like (Okada, 1976).

It also has been found that textbooks contain many inaccuracies and inaccurate characterizations of Asians and Asian-Americans. An extensive review of high school social studies textbooks showed that Asiatic minorities, such as those of Chinese and Japanese origin, were frequently treated in a manner implying they were racially inferior. None of the 45 texts examined gave fair treatment in terms of factual information on Americans of Asiatic origin compared to that accorded other groups in this country (Kane, 1970). Recently, the Elementary and Secondary Education Act (ESEA) Title VII: *The Bilingual Education Act* has been generating interest in development of more racially fair and positive instructional materials for school-aged children, the effect of which will be felt at some time.

Teachers are not only the major source of referral to the School Based Support Team, but are also the ones who play an integral role in establishing norms of appropriate and inappropriate behavior in children by acting or not acting on certain classroom behavior of the children. With respect to the present concern about passivity and invisibility of the Asian immigrant, teachers are in a unique position to counteract such racial stereotype-inspired expectations or to permit it to continue.

REFERRAL DISCOURAGING EDUCATIONAL POLICIES

The Bureau of Child Guidance (BCG), the predecessor of the present day's School Based Support Team (SBST) until 1980, actively discouraged the referrals on immigrant children who have not been in this country at least two years. It was in the hope that the majority of these children would make successful transition into the American way of life with the second language acquisition and cultural assimilation. Administration of tests and provision of Special Education programs were severely curtailed except in cases of physical handicaps. This practice, although rooted in optimism and humanitarian concerns, probably deterred many legitimate referrals, resulting in failure of early identification of important psychoeducational problems and resultant inattention to the needs of these immigrant children.

The School Based Support Team, responding not so much to the humanitarian tradition of its predecessor but to the 1980s Zeitgeist— "Mainstreaming" pays little attention to the immigrant children. These children are expected to function in "the least restrictive environment"—considering that this environment is, in most cases, not a bilingual and/or bicultural classroom with supportive services, and thus is the *most* restrictive environment. Some parents of these children actually prefer this monolingual English-speaking, "regular" classroom without supportive services for their children, thinking that throwing them into the river will teach them how to swim more quickly than placing them in a sequentially arranged instructional program. This practice, although highly debatable, can easily be understood in light of the fact that assimilation rather than isolation is the predominant adaptive mood of Asian immigrant groups and that some impatient immigrants are willing and eager to become absorbed into the mainstream of American life as quickly as possible. Many of these children manage to swim or to stay afloat without displaying overt signs of mental anguish; some fail to accomplish either and these children eventually come to the attention of the school mental health personnel after having suffered major learning and adjustment failures.

Apart from the philosophical considerations, there is a real and practical limitation in the capacity of the educational system in assessing Asian immigrant children's psycho-educational needs and in providing necessary supportive programs. Unavailability of bilingual and/or bicultural staff makes it virtually impossible to carry out meaningful services for these children. To this author's knowledge, out of approximately 800 psychologists and social workers, only 1 bilingual Korean-American, 1 Chinese-American, 1 Filipino-American school psychologist, and 1 Japanese-American, and 1 Pakistani school social worker are working in the New York City public school system. The Public Law 94-142 mandates psychological examination of school children be carried out in the child's dominant language, creating highly desirable but impossible situations for these children.

The bilingual education program attempts to provide educational opportunities for children who are unable to participate in the learning process because of their inability to function effectively in the English language. This is being done by providing instruction in the student's dominant language while at the same time providing intensive English language instruction. Asian immigrant students attending a school where a sizeable (5% or more) group of students whose mother tongue is an Asian language are entitled to bilingual instruction. Limited availability of quaiified teachers and ambivalence of the parents about bilingual education hamper the program's efforts.

IMPLICATIONS AND RECOMMENDATIONS

Despite the insurmountable difficulties which Asian immigrant children are subjected to in our schools including, but not limited to, problems of second language acquisition, cultural assimilation, and psychological adjustment, these children remain largely invisible and their many and varied needs largely unmet. Although the School Based Support Team should be the most logical choice for psycho-educational intervention for these children as children of all nationality backgrounds, they come to the school to face the challenge of "making it" in this country. These children rarely come to the attention of the Team. Major factors contributing to the conspicuously low referral rate have been examined in the context of (1) referral inhibiting characteristics of the children; (2) stereotype-inspired expectations of the teachers; and (3) referral discouraging educational policies.

Meaningful programs to meet the multi-faceted problems should be multi-disciplinary, multi-level, and bilingual and bicultural in nature. The following recommendations are being made:

1. As much as possible, the School Based Support Team, in collaboration with bilingual and bicultural community workers, should direct its attention to the needs of immigrant children. The central school board office should launch outreach efforts to locate qualified bilingual and bicultural psychologists, social workers, and educational evaluators in Asian communities, and provide training programs for future professionals in these areas. Also, the educational system, in collaboration with professional and academic communities of psychology and education, should endeavor to develop

and refine psychometric tools which can be used to assess the psycho-educational needs of the immigrant children.

2. Consciousness-raising groups should be organized for the school teachers and other school personnel to examine and explore how they may be contributing to the unmet needs of Asian immigrant children and to the perpetuation of Asian stereotypes of passivity, conformity, etc. Recently, massive efforts have been made to raise the New York City school teachers' consciousness in their prejudicial dealings with the black and Hispanic children by providing "Lora training" workshops. This has been an effort to raise the consciousness that children of these two minority groups have been dealt with unfairly in the educational processes due to the teachers' failure to recognize these children's needs and rights. Similar workshops for the teachers with respect to Asian-American and immigrant children should also be given in the schools where these populations are found in large numbers.

3. Assertive training programs might be implemented in a school setting for some Asian-American and/or Asian immigrant children who need to learn a more assertive mode of coping and how to discard some of their passive behavior patterns. These children may be subjected to experiences and opportunities which stimulate their ability to express themselves, to assert their opinions and rights, to make independent decisions, and to assume leadership roles. In light of their language barrier and/or deficiency, this might best be carried out in bilingual and bicultural settings.

REFERENCES

Bourne, P. G. The Chinese student—acculturation and mental illness. *Psychiatry,* 1975, *38,* 269-277.

Chang, T. S. The self-concept of children in ethnic groups: Black American and Korean American. *The Elementary School Journal,* 1975, *76*(1), 52-58.

Chu, R. *Majors of Chinese and Japanese students at the University of California, Berkeley for the past 20 years.* Project Report, AS 150, Asian Study Division, Berkeley, California. University of California-Berkeley, 1971.

Deutsch, M., & Collins, M. E. The effect of public policy in housing projects upon interracial attitudes. In G. E. Swanson, T. E. Newcomb, & E. L. Harteley (Eds.), *Readings in social psychology.* New York: Holt, 1952.

Kane, M. B. *Minorities in textbooks.* Chicago: Quadrangle Books, 1970.

Kim, Y. J. *The relation of dogmatism and prejudice of the teacher to race and sex stereotyping of Asian-American children.* Unpublished doctoral dissertation. New York University, 1980.

Kuroiwa, P. The invisible students. *Momentum.* October, 1975.

Meredith, G. M. Amae and acculturation among Japanese-American college students in Hawaii. *The Journal of Social Psychology,* 1966, *70,* 171-180.

Okada, A. How children's books distort the Asian-American image. In *The portrayal of Asian Americans in children's books,* a special booklet for the interracial books for children, *Bulletin,* 1976, 7, 2, 3.

Parady, J. M. What teachers believe, what children achieve. *Elementary School Journal,* 1969, *69,* 370-374.

Rothenthal, R., & Jacobson, L. *Pygmalion in the classroom.* New York: Holt, Rinehart & Winston, 1968.

Sue, D. W., & Kirk, B. A. Psychological characteristics of Chinese-American students. *Journal of Counseling Psychology,* 1973, *85,* 131-136.

Watanabe, C. Self-expression and the Asian-American experience. *Personnel and Guidance Journal,* 1973, *51*(6), 390-396.